DEAREST MAMA

DEAREST
MAMA

The Lost Letters of a Fallen Soldier and the Stories of Those He Left Behind

★ ★ ★ ★ ★ ★ ★ ★ ★

WILLIAM S. WALKER

THE UNIVERSITY OF
SOUTH CAROLINA PRESS

© 2024 University of South Carolina

Published by the University of South Carolina Press
Columbia, South Carolina 29208

uscpress.com

Printed in the United States of America

Library of Congress Cataloging-in-Publication Data
can be found at https://lccn.loc.gov/2024031211

ISBN: 978-1-64336-502-2 (paperback)
ISBN: 978-1-64336-503-9 (ebook)

Author's note. Original spelling and punctuation
in the letters have been maintained.

To the best of the best—the men and women of the US Armed Forces and to all the veterans who have worn the uniform of our country over the years. Thank you for your service.

CONTENTS

LIST OF ILLUSTRATIONS

Prologue

Last year I found a packet of letters that solved an enduring mystery in my family. The letters were written by my uncle, Private First Class Fletcher Blanton, a World War II US Army infantryman killed in action in Germany in January 1945. Until those letters were discovered our family knew little about his life in the Army and death in combat.

My uncle's wartime letters home were stored for decades in a brown paper grocery bag tucked away in an antique oak pie safe.[1] I found the letters on a summer morning in 2022 in my garage attic when I opened the cobweb-covered cabinet that had been shoved against a side wall many years earlier. As I pulled the cabinet doors open, the overfilled, disintegrating paper bag fell into my arms. Inside the bag I found a penciled note in my father's oversized scrawl. He had written: "Bill SAVE THIS BAG. PAPERS. Go through these before you throw away. 1986." Under that note were hundreds of family photos and official papers and at the bottom a stack of letters in a small, timeworn candy box.

The note alone from my father was a shock since he had been dead thirty-five years. It was written at a time when he and I had tried to put his affairs in order and clean out the accumulated debris of forty years of living in the family home. That came in 1986 after a doctor told us my dad's cancer was incurable. And that it would be best for both of us to manage for the inevitable. That meant I needed to come home from my reporting post in Germany to help him clean the small five-room apartment above our former streetcorner grocery store in the small town of Nichols, South Carolina. The place had been the Walker family home since 1948. I had not lived there in nearly twenty years and the apartment, once neat and clean, had slowly fallen into disorder in the fifteen years since my mother's death.

Apparently, sometime during that 1986 cleanup, my dad found the bag and, without telling me, wrote the note, then put everything in the pie safe

Figure 1. An old chocolate box held Bud Blanton's
letters home. Collection of the author.

and duct-taped it closed. My father died less than two years later, and the cabinet eventually came to be stored in my upstairs garage, a few miles outside of Nichols. By my calculation the bag had been undisturbed in the pie safe for thirty-six years and the oldest photos and papers dated back more than a century.

I sat down in a rocking chair in the middle of the garage attic and dumped the contents of the bag onto the floor. On top were dozens of photographs, some dating from my dad's time in the US Navy in World War II. There were photos of my mother as a young farm girl in Horry County, South Carolina. And snapshots from past decades of our little hometown of Nichols that showed some of its 300 residents and scenes of everyday life in the Pee Dee region along the northeast corner of South Carolina.

Under the stack of photographs and a thick pile of official-looking papers I found half of a battered Russell McPhail chocolates box filled with letters and postcards. The letters were written mostly on flimsy paper or were miniature V-Mail letters from World War II. All were from Private First Class Fletcher Blanton, my mother's oldest brother, the only immediate family member killed in World War II. The first piece of paper at the top of the stack was a postcard-sized V-Mail letter. My uncle, who everyone in the family called Bud, had written:

Dec. 5, 1944
In Germany
Dearest Mama
How are you and all the family. I am okay only I am so full. We get more to eat than we can eat. I haven't gotten any mail from anyone yet but I don't think it will be so long before I hear from you. I wrote you yesterday and I also wrote Dot. Today is a cold fair day. It snowed some yesterday. I bet you couldnt guess what I did yesterday. I took a bath. that was the first bath I have had since I have been over here. I havent had a hair cut since a week before I left the states. I have been trying to get it cut but no one seems to cut hair. There is no place to spend my money over here. I havent been paid yet. I am going to send this money home when I get paid if there is any way. Tell ever body hello an write me often. I may not write often but dont worry for I want have time to write much. I am the youngest pvt in my company. Love an Luck Bud

I thumbed through the box of more than three dozen letters, cards, and notes. The overseas letters all included Bud Blanton's address as a member of Co. D, 413th Infantry, which was part of the 104th Infantry Division, the Timberwolves. For the next hour I read many of the letters and cards. I learned that my uncle had been drafted in early 1944 as a 19-year-old and went to basic training at Camp Blanding in Florida. He reached Europe by troop ship in autumn 1944 and was on the front lines for less than two months before his death. The last letter in the stack was dated January 9, 1945, the day before he was killed.

Before I found the letters, I had known my uncle only from his picture in uniform during basic training. Over the years I had seen framed copies of that photo hung in all the homes of his seven siblings, my aunts and uncles. And I stood with my mother many times before his tombstone in the Blanton family cemetery in Horry County. From earliest remembrance I always recognized his name and knew he was my mother's revered, dead brother. But beyond that, almost nothing.

Figure 2. Fletcher "Bud" Blanton's Army Photo, 1944. Collection of the Author.

There, in the garage attic, I read through the final year of Bud Blanton's life. In his wartime letters he expressed his loneliness and poured out his heart, literally begging his seven brothers and sisters to write him every day. I learned he had a girlfriend named Dot. She had been mentioned in that first letter I read and in nearly every other letter he wrote. There was a small photo of her amid the stack of letters. In the autumn and winter of 1944, she had written him often, sometimes three letters a day. It was clear from his writing that her letters lifted his spirits and meant the world to him. However, there was not a single one of her letters in the box. Who was she? I had to find out. In one letter he asked about a boyhood friend, Hayden, who was also a soldier. What happened to him? Could he still be alive? Another letter asked if the money he sent home had been received. In another letter he asked if the family could send him a pork shoulder and some good things to eat from my grandmother's kitchen so he, too, would have something to share with the other soldiers.

Bud Blanton never finished high school and his writing was rough, the punctuation often nonexistent. But he was more than capable of expressing his hopes and dreams and fears. And he ended nearly all his letters and cards with a request for mail. His favorite closing message on the cards and letters was *Love an Luck Bud.*

He had been born Fletcher Stanley Blanton, Jr. in rural Dillon County, South Carolina, on Nov. 26, 1924. He was the oldest of three sons born to my grandmother, Jessie Mae Graham Blanton, and her husband Fletcher. In 1944, when Bud went to the Army, the rest of the family unit was his widowed 41-year-old mother, five sisters, and two brothers. The sisters were Vera (born 1916), Edna (1919), my mother Clarise (1921), Betty (1927), and Sally (1929). His brothers were Carol (1933), who the family called Son, and Ralph (1936).

Jessie Mae Graham and Fletcher Stanley Blanton had married in 1915 and endured the Great Depression as sharecroppers on a local landowner's small tobacco farm in a sparsely settled section of Horry County close to the North Carolina line. At that time, local land could be purchased for a few dollars an acre. And tracts of the unwanted, barren, sandy ridges and depressions along the coast at Myrtle Beach, thirty-five miles distant, sold for pennies an acre. However, few local people had even pennies to spare. Bud's father, my grandfather, was a hard worker and an even harder drinker. When my uncle was 15 in 1940, his father died at the age of 48. Cause of death was listed as a cerebral hemorrhage. But my mother was always convinced the hemorrhage was brought on by the heavy drinking, and she was a fierce, lifelong opponent of alcoholic beverages of any sort.

The widowed mother, Jessie Mae, was left with almost no income to raise her eight children. Bud dropped out of school that year after finishing the 9th grade and took over the heavy work on the farm owned by Jim and Sarah Ann Floyd. The Floyds lived nearby in Duford, a crossroads settlement of perhaps fifty people in Horry County along SC Highway 9. The biggest town in the area was Nichols, a prosperous community of 250 people five miles away across the Lumber River in neighboring Marion County. Thus, most everyone living around the Duford area like the Blantons received their mail on Rural Route 2, Nichols, South Carolina.

Shortly before Bud Blanton was drafted into the Army in 1944, my grandmother gave up the farm and moved her family into a small, wood frame house on the unpaved back street of Nichols. Daughters Betty and Sally and sons Ralph and Carol, still lived with her. Betty was a senior at Floyds High School in Duford and commuted with a teacher daily to Floyds until the end of the school year. Like her sister Clarise seven years earlier, Betty was on the way to becoming class valedictorian. Sally, a 10th grader, transferred to Nichols High School. Vera, Edna, and Clarise had already married and lived outside the home. Vera was in Fayetteville, NC, while Edna and Clarise were nearby in Nichols. Jessie Mae Blanton took in sewing and her children living at home did any available jobs that paid.

It was from Nichols that Bud Blanton went off to the Army and eventually to the war in Europe. And it was to the Blanton home in Nichols that the telegram from the War Department announcing his death was delivered in January 1945.

In 2022, when I found the letters, only one Blanton sibling remained alive, my 95-year-old aunt, Betty Mincey. I called that evening and asked what she knew about the letters.

"Nothing," she answered. "I've never seen them but I sure want to read them. I do remember that there were six or seven boys killed from our area in the war about the same time as Bud."

I did not know that, I told her.

A day later I brought the box to her and her husband, C. P., the World War II sailor she married in 1944 while a senior in high school. He was the same C. P. Mincey who my Uncle Bud wrote about in one of his letters, questioning if C. P. would be a good match for my aunt. Seventy-eight years of marriage later, Bud Blanton's question was easily answered. The Minceys were still happily together with an ever-growing group of great grandchildren. And their oldest son and a great grandson were named Fletcher like my uncle and grandfather.

I knew from family stories that Bud Blanton had been killed sometime during the Battle of the Bulge, the last great German offensive of World War II. And that until he went to war, he had never been far from home. From a first reading of the letters, I learned that in the Army he saw England, France, Belgium, the Netherlands, and Germany. And, in total, he spent a little over two months at war in Europe before being killed in action.

I knew also from my mother that my uncle's remains rested for nearly four years with thousands of other fallen comrades at the US military

Figure 3. Fletcher Blanton's gravestone, Blanton Cemetery,
Horry County, South Carolina. Photo by the author.

cemetery in Margraten, Holland. I had visited with her there once in 1970. The documents in the box of letters revealed the paperwork my mother filled out for the family, enabling the repatriation of my uncle's remains from Margraten in November 1948 to the Blanton family cemetery a few miles from Duford.

The day after finding the letters I drove out to the Blanton Cemetery in Horry County to read the inscription on my uncle's granite tombstone.

PFC. FLETCHER BLANTON, Co. D, 413 INF. TIMBER WOLF DIVISION
NOV. 26, 1924
JAN. 10, 1945
KILLED IN ACTION IN GERMANY
WORLD WAR 2
GAVE HIS LIFE FOR THE CAUSE OF LIBERTY
THY WILL BE DONE

In my professional life I spent nearly thirty years overseas as a reporter and editor for the newspaper *Stars and Stripes*[2] and all too often witnessed family loss as modern-day soldiers, sailors, marines, airmen, and civilians were honored after giving their lives for their country. And over the years I covered Memorial Day and Veterans Day and D-Day ceremonies at American Battle Monuments Commission cemeteries all over Europe. Those who never made it home are interred in immaculately maintained cemeteries run by the Battle Monuments Commission.

Through the years I always felt my stories were never sufficient to honor the last, final sacrifice I saw embodied in the precisely aligned rows of markers, the seemingly unending lines of Latin crosses and Stars of David. Now, in my seventh decade, with far fewer years ahead than behind me, my uncle's letters provided the most poignant reminder of service to country I had ever known, the letters from the one soldier whose wartime experience is an inseparable part of my own heritage. I asked myself if there were something I could write about Fletcher Blanton's life that might speak to those who have never faced such a loss and offer comfort to those who have.

My aunt had spoken of at least six other soldiers from the Nichols area who had been killed in World War II around the time of my uncle's death. Who were they? Where were they buried? Did they have family remaining? Over the coming months, with the help of Betty Mincey's son Charles Fletcher Mincey, I came to know a great deal about the lives of my uncle and the other young, local men who died while in the service of their country.

I also thought it important to include not only excerpts from my uncle's letters but also transcriptions of all the letters and postcards written home and saved. The transcriptions are exactly as they were written with his capitalization and spelling. No corrections were made. In addition, many chapters begin with excerpts from letters and written commentary by fellow soldiers in the Timberwolf Division.

In total, more than 400,000 American families received the same War Department death notice as my grandmother during World War II. This book about her son's life and the other veterans killed in action from my home area is intended to honor all men and women who served and, most importantly, to commemorate the lives of those who ultimately gave all. They must never be forgotten.

William S. Walker

Fork Retch, South Carolina
Summer 2024

CHAPTER 1

A Sister Remembers

Ninety-seven-year-old Betty Blanton Mincey is the last living person who truly knew Bud Blanton. She is his sister, the only surviving child of Fletcher and Jessie Mae Blanton. She remembers her brother as a happy, fun-loving boy in a close-knit farm family that struggled to survive the poverty of the Great Depression.

"He was the oldest boy," Betty Mincey said. "He always went with Daddy to the store. We had an old car and the store was at Duford, about a mile away from the farm. He always treated Bud to a nickel bag of candy and my sister Sally and I were always after his candy when he got home. He followed his daddy around everywhere. When Bud was about sixteen, Daddy got sick. He was sick two or three months. They said it was some kind of dysentery but I think it was probably cirrhosis of the liver. Back then they didn't identify things like that. When he passed away it put more responsibility on all of us. Bud was our instructor. He was the manager. He told everybody what to do.[1]

"My sister Clarise and Will Walker were courting. They had gotten married but they didn't tell anyone. My oldest sister Vera sort of took over and helped Momma when Daddy died in 1940. My sister Edna was smart, and she did things also. Shortly after Daddy died Clarise moved to Nichols after they announced they were married.

"Vera and Edna started dating people from around Nichols. Vera dated John E. Elvington and Edna dated Hubert Scott. Vera married John E. and moved to Nichols before Mama moved us there. Edna married Hubert and he became chief of police in Nichols. That left Mama and Sally and Son and Ralph and Bud and me at home.

"Mama farmed for three years after Daddy died. They drafted Bud so we had to quit farming and moved to Nichols in 1944. Mama never forgave the draft board for taking him. She needed him on the farm. I don't

*Figure 4. Betty Blanton Mincey,
1944, before her brother Bud's death.
Collection of the author.*

remember how far Bud got in school.[2] I think he must have dropped out of school before he was drafted. Hayden Floyd was his friend and he got killed in World War II also."

"What do you remember about your brother?" I asked Betty Mincey.

"He was a typical young boy," she said. "A little on the wild side when he was growing up. You could see he wasn't real settled. It settled him down when he went into service. He was like most 17- and 18-year-olds. My husband C. P. said he was something of a rounder."

"Bud got his training in Florida and when he came home he looked very good in uniform," she continued. "He was in shape. He was handsome in his uniform. He was not as tall as Ralph (his youngest brother) was going to be, maybe five nine or ten. He was always cutting up, making faces at himself in the mirror. He always wore a cap. A baseball type cap. He would wear it to bed and momma would take it off of him."

He had a steady girlfriend before he went to the Army, Betty Mincey said. "He was dating Dot Floyd," she said. "Her father was Jessie Floyd and they lived on the Lake View highway out of Nichols.

Figure 5. Bud Blanton's father, Horry County farmer Fletcher Blanton. Collection of the author.

"We knew her. She sort of ran in my and my sister Sally's circles. Sometimes we would go to the movies in Mullins and if you had extra money, you would get a hamburger at Mike's Place beside the movie theater. If you didn't have the money, you just got a coke. It was a treat to go to the movies. Mike Petros had three beautiful girls and the boys would all go there just to get a hamburger and see the Petros girls."[3]

"I don't remember when Bud got his draft notice," Betty Mincey continued. "We were distressed when he had to go because we knew we couldn't farm anymore. Our farm was probably a fifty-acre farm and we had eleven acres of tobacco. That was the only cash crop that we had. Although we had an old car, we really had no money. Once, my sister Sally and I found a penny at the house. We walked a mile all the way to Duford to the store. We told the man behind the counter there, Mr. Lambert, I think, that we wanted to buy a five-cent candy bag and showed him the penny. And he gave us the candy. When Daddy came to the store later, Mr. Lambert told him about us and he paid the other four cents.

Figure 6. Jessie Mae Graham Blanton, mother of Bud Blanton, ca. 1950. Collection of the author.

"I got married in November 1944 and C. P. was in the Navy. He went back to the Navy in Norfolk and I stayed at our house. I remember that summer Bud writing from Camp Blanding in Florida. He wrote that the boys would get blisters on their feet. When he came back from training, he was more settled. And he had a girlfriend. He dated Winnie Floyd but Dot Floyd was his regular. She once told us she felt real close to us because of that. They might have gotten married or they might not have if he had come back. People change when they go off. He came home in the fall, probably October. And then they shipped him out right on over there. He had on his winter uniform when he left, I remember."

C. P. Mincey said, "Bud was a jolly person. He acted like he was happy all the time. He was like most of us. He was a little on the wild side."

The thing her brother loved most once he became a soldier was writing letters and receiving mail, Betty Mincey said. "He wrote to everybody. He wrote to Momma every day. It was obvious that he had his mind on home. I was so young that I didn't realize that he might not get back home. When you are young you don't realize there is that much danger. Then we found out the casualties were bad. Four or five boys from here got killed during that time. They didn't come back. And then Bud didn't come back either."

She said reading the letters for the first time in 2022 gave her an opportunity to know her brother as a man. "I was young then and after reading the letters," she said, "I can see he was a good son. In the letters he wrote that when he got back, he hoped he could run a store. He felt responsible for Mama and the boys. You could see he had really grown up. Through the letters I got to know his thoughts and what kind of person he had become. When I read those letters, it was like my brother had come back from the dead. I was reliving the past."

CHAPTER 2

From the Farm to the Front Line

Voices From Bud Blanton's 104th Infantry Division
I think, too, about the differences of being "citizen soldiers" in
wartime as opposed to the business of being a professional military
person. Especially, I remember how everyone in Company L got
along; how during ordinary training programs rank was observed
but otherwise everyone was pretty much equal. It was essentially a
recognition that we were all in the same boat, so let's get on with it
and get the job done.

—*Mel Falck, Company L, 414th Infantry Regiment*

I move along a gray Belgian road, part of a long line of olive drab,
heading toward the horizon and the sound of distant guns. I am not
afraid! I am too ignorant for that! Like my comrades, I am anxious
lest I fail to measure up when the test arrives. None of us says much,
each absorbed in his own private world. Then the agonized lowing
of unmilked dairy cattle assaults our ears, and those muted screams
set my teeth on edge. It is a blessed relief to pass out of earshot, only
now the muttering of the guns grows louder. Backpacks and bed-
rolls, mine among them, begin to litter the road. I need only tooth
brush and razor to supplement the tools of war I carry.

—*W. Robert Nolan, Company I, 413th Infantry Regiment*

Bud Blanton's relatively uncomplicated life as a teenager literally ended
the moment he walked into a small office in Conway, South Carolina, on

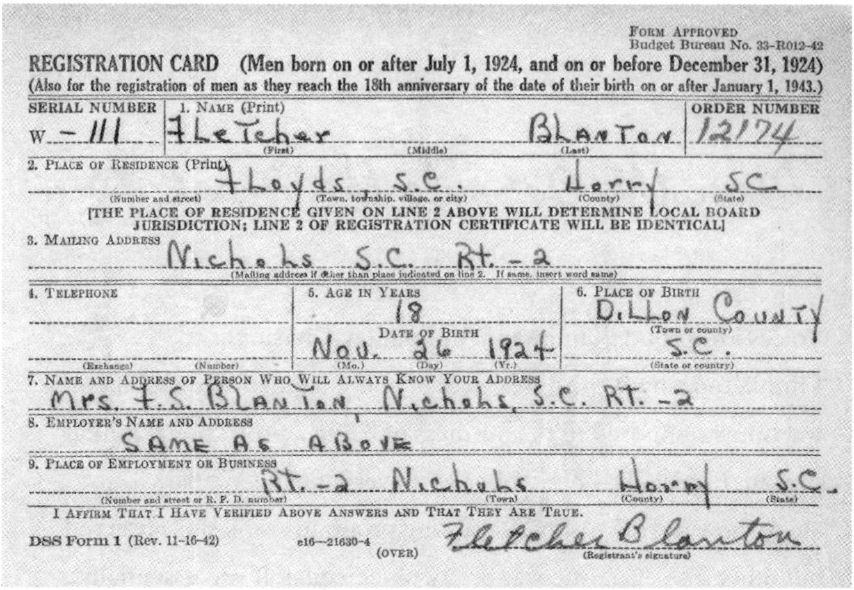

Figure 7. Fletcher Blanton's draft registration card,
December 28, 1942. Collection of the author.

December 28, 1942. There, he registered for the draft, the national system enacted September 16, 1940, as the Selective Service Training and Service Act.[1]

He verified on the card filled out for local board Registrar Ruby W. Williams that he was a resident of Rural Route 2, Nichols and lived in Horry County. He had turned 18 on November 26 and was complying with the regulation to register with a draft board. He gave his height as 5 feet, 8 inches and weight as 135 pounds. He had blue eyes, brown hair, and a light complexion.[2] Although he was the only fulltime working male on the Blanton family farm and the only worker capable of performing the heaviest farm tasks, my uncle probably knew he would be drafted into military service. That was the likely future of every able-bodied young man from his area who chose not to volunteer.

In total, over 10 million American men would be conscripted during the war and Bud Blanton's number came up in early 1944. It was a notice feared by his mother, who knew the life of the family would change forever when her son was taken away. Without Bud at home, the family would have to abandon farming, the only life they had known. She also knew that he might never come back from the war. The newspaper accounts of US servicemen being killed in North Africa and the Pacific began appearing regularly in 1942.

"We needed him to do the heavy work," his sister Betty Blanton Mincey said. "We grew tobacco and he did the big things that had to be done. He told the rest of us what we needed to do. At that time my brother Son was 10 and my other brother Ralph was 8. Momma knew we couldn't do it without him.My mother never told anyone but us, but she felt like the draft board wanted to make an example of Bud. He worked on the farm, but he was out there after work riding around with his friends, doing things."[3]

"He was definitely a rounder, he got out and had a good time when he wasn't working on the farm," said Betty Mincey's husband, C. P. He had known Bud as a classmate at Floyds High School until Bud dropped out. C. P. continued through graduation, then volunteered for the US Navy in 1944.[4]

"Momma thought they wanted to make an example of Bud and draft him," Betty Mincey recalled. "But she never told anyone outside the family."

His notice came in the spring of 1944, a momentous year in the war on the world stage and equally so for the families around Nichols and throughout the country. Everywhere, young men were being called up to fill the expanding manpower requirements of the US military.

In the headlines, General Dwight D. Eisenhower assumed command of the European Theater in January. The battle to take the German stronghold of Monte Cassino and drive the Nazis out of Italy began. The US Navy advanced steadily across the Pacific, attacking Guam, Saipan, and Tinian in the Marianas and invading the Admiralty Islands. The D-Day landings in Normandy were carried out successfully in June, the liberation of Paris followed in August, and the march across Europe continued in the months after that.

My uncle's journey to war really began when he dropped his duffel bag in the barracks floor at Camp Blanding, Florida, in the summer of 1944. The sprawling 30,000-acre military camp about forty miles west of St. Augustine had been established in 1939 to train soldiers for war. From 1940 until 1943 whole Army divisions were trained there including the 1st Infantry Division, the famed Big Red One, and the 29th Infantry Division, known for its courageous role in the D-Day landing at Omaha Beach.[5]

By the time Bud Blanton reached Camp Blanding, the cadre there had ceased to train full divisions. The training by then focused on preparing soldiers for duty as replacements primarily in combat units. Bud would be one of those replacements, eventually assigned to the 104th Infantry Division, the Timberwolf Division from Washington State.

My uncle had been used to working from sunup to sunset on a South Carolina tobacco farm for most of his life, and the basic training at Camp Blanding did not faze him much, at least according to his cards and letters home. Being outdoors was normal for him. He thought the bivouacs in the forest, the night maneuvers, and the time spent in a tent were a lot like camping out in Horry County as a boy. It was at Camp Blanding that he began the cards and letters to his mother and sisters and brothers. His correspondence was somewhat brief and his grammar at times spotty. But nearly every message gave him an opportunity to express how much he cared for everyone at home and for home itself. Not the house in Nichols but the one on the Wannamaker Church Road down the crossroads from Duford, where he had spent an impoverished but happy youth. Above all, he was homesick. Prior to the Army he had never been more than a day's car drive from the family farm. A trip of even a few miles to nearby Mullins or Conway was a long one for him.

On July 2 he wrote his mother:

> I bet you are cooking Dinner while I am writing this letter. I would like to be at home to eat dinner today. It sure is lonesome up here on Sunday. I hate to see Sunday come. When I am working, I don't think much about going home but when Sunday comes I sure want to go home.

His military pay was approximately $50 a month and from the beginning he tried to send a portion of it home. That left him short of money, but he found a solution. In mid-July he wrote, "I washed a few clothes for some boys tonight. They pay plenty an I am going to need the money anyway an I dont mind washing them. Write soon an be good. Love Bud."

The intensity of the work, as he called combat training, increased almost daily. Midway his training he wrote:

> The Captain told us today that we were to get up at 5 o clock tomorrow morning an go out in the woods an practice close combat

until 2 oclock Saturday morning before day. He said that would be the hardest day in our cicle.

He closed that letter with these words: "I want all of you to be sure to write the next two weeks for I will be camping out. Love Bud."

In the Army he got all the food he wanted, although he wrote it did not measure up to his mother's home cooking. He also got new clothes, something unusual for him, and he wrote proudly:

All of my clothes I have got in the Army are new. Some of the boys got clothes that had been worn before. . . . A nice field jacket if they let me keep it. They may take . . . our summer clothes before we leave here. But we get another coat before we leave I think.

They reached the most intense phase of their training by mid-September, but it didn't seem to bother him, particularly the long marches. He wrote:

there is nobody here that can march any farther than I can. I never been so tired since I been here that I couldn't march 2 miles more. I haven't had a blister on my feet since I have been in the Army. Some of the boys had blisters on their feet. An they had to keep marching on the blisters on their feet. An the blisters on their feet burst and make sores. Now they have sores on their feet and have to make the 25 mile hike like that.

Shortly before the end of his time at Camp Blanding, he wrote: "I only have 3 more weeks. I will be glad when tomorrow comes for it time to start back to work and the more days I work the less time we have to stay . . . ."

He came home to Nichols after training in the autumn and his sister Betty remembered the day he walked into the house. "He was handsome in his uniform. I remember him as tall and slim, never heavy." He could not tell his family where he was being shipped to because he didn't know. They guessed it would be the European theater because that was where most of the local young men were being sent.[6]

When he walked out the door after his military leave, Betty Mincey recalled it was the last time any of them would ever see him alive. "We didn't think about things like that then," she said. "We were young. We didn't know about war. We just thought he would come back to us. But he didn't."[7]

After he left Nichols, Bud Blanton spent a single day with his sister Vera in Fayetteville, North Carolina, en route to his next duty station. An undated postcard written to Vera with a Baltimore scene on the front side appears to be from late September 1944. He wrote:

> I wonder what you are doing tonight. I have been writing Mama an Dot. I haven't had very much time to write while I have been here. I will write you a long letter when I get to my next camp. I am leaving in the morning. I guess I will be in France in a week an a half. I enjoyed staying that day with you very much. I have to close now. Bye Love Bud.

The unit Bud Blanton was to eventually join in November, the 413th Infantry Regiment of the Timberwolf Division, crossed the Atlantic before him in the last week of August 1944 in a fifty-six-ship convoy. Large elements of the division traveled aboard the *USS Lejeune,* a former German cargo ship converted to a Navy troop transport.[8]

Four ships carried the bulk of the Timberwolf Division across the Atlantic. They were the *USS George Washington,* the *USS Lejeune,* the *USAT Cristobal,* and the *SS Ocean Mail.*[9]

Bud was to serve in Company D, and one of the soldiers from Company A described his unit's arrival in France. "Our troopship, the *USS Lejeune,* brought us to the ruined port of Cherbourg, France, on September 7, 1944," wrote Private First Class Nile R. Blood.[10] "From there we were transported by trucks to an apple orchard a little south of the village of Valognes in the Normandy peninsula. The area was largely rolling pastureland and apple orchards."

Nile Blood summarized the coming months for himself, Bud Blanton, and the rest of the 413th Infantry:

> the apple trees in the orchard were infested with the parasite plant, mistletoe. Both the holly and the mistletoe are traditionally used for Christmas decorations. However, the timing was wrong. By Christmas, we were on the west side of the flooded Roer River near Düren, Germany, and were veterans of much intense combat

in Holland and Germany. The German Ardennes offensive (the Battle of the Bulge) was underway just to south of our position.[11]

A week later the bulk of the division left the orchard at Valognes and marched thirty-two miles down the rural middle of the Cotentin Peninsula to the railhead at La Haye-du-Puits. A Timberwolf Division medic, Paul Marshall, wrote:

> This was undoubtedly the hardest march any of us had undertaken, even in the days of hard training. We carried our full field packs, rifles and all, leaving the apple orchards at daylight and finally ending up, yes, in another apple orchard around six in the evening, where we once again pitched our pup tents and without hesitation, fell immediately to sleep.[12]

Marshall treated dozens of soldiers for severe blisters and even worse, he said, were those whose inner thighs were rubbed to raw flesh by the wool trousers some unit members had been issued in the United States.

Excluding the long march, most of the Timberwolves had fond memories of Normandy. Paul Marshall recalled being greeted by French people "as we marched through the small villages along the way."

> They made me feel like a conquering hero just a bit. Of course, we had only a canteen of water to last us for the day, so when they stood there handing out glasses and bottles of cider to us we were foolish not to take them, much to the chagrin of many who overdid it and found themselves with stomachaches and even instant diarrhea from an overdosing of cider.[13]

At the railhead the division was put aboard train cars for the journey to the front. Only the top commander, Major General Terry de la Mesa Allen, and his staff knew the 104th would enter the war on the front line in the Netherlands and Belgium in the coming weeks. Daniel Ponzevic, a member of the Division's Company C, 329th Engineer Battalion, described the move:

> We found our way through France and into Belgium through Brussels, which the British and Canadians had liberated, into

bivouac until the "Brass" decided where we would get accli-
mated to combat and properly "blooded." I do not like the term
"blooded" since it means casualties. Since our General Terry Allen
had some experience with the British in Africa, their meetings
were probably very correct. It was ironic that we were going to be
placed in combat as part of the First Canadian Army, relieving the
British 49th.[14]

After an approximately two-week stay in a temporary camp, the 104th
moved into the front line in the area around Wuustwezel, Belgium, north
of Antwerp and a few miles south of the Dutch border astride the road to
Breda, Holland. Henry Vigdor, a member of Company B, 329th Engineer
Battalion recalled:

We were taking up positions occupied by the previous troops.
Suddenly the Germans started shelling us and we immediately
started jumping into the vacated foxholes. After jumping into "my
hole" another G.I. came flying in on top of me. I hollered "go find
your own hole." The G.I. patted me on the helmet and said, "Take
it easy sonny boy." I looked up to see who it was and saw a star on
his helmet. It was Brigadier General Moore, the Assistant Division
C.O. The shelling stopped and the general took off without saying
goodbye. At least I can say I hung out with the "big boys."[15]

From his letters we know Bud and the other replacements were on
their way to the 104th during this time. And we have to think that their
route into France and across the country was similar to that encountered
by the main part of the division six weeks earlier. On November 23 he
wrote his mother he was in Normandy. Two days later he wrote:

I am still in France. I was in England at one time. I sure hope I
hear from you soon. But I guess it will be a long time before I do
hear from home. I wonder how the war is getting along now. I dont
ever hear any war news now for I can't read french papers. We cant
spend very much money over hear. All we can buy is 2 packs of
cigarettes a week an 2 bars of candy.

In that letter he showed the immense change the Army had made in his outlook on life.

> I think you can buy wine an sider in town but I am not ever going to start back drinking so I can save most of the money I get while I am over here for I no I will need some money when I get back home. I am hoping this war will hurry an stop for I no lots of the boys are being killed. I want to stay over here until the war is over for if I ever go back to the states I wouldn't come back. I visited La Havre France not long ago. Mama there is lots of things that I would like to tell you. But it would be cut out by the cinsor.

My uncle had no way of knowing it but one of those boys killed had been his best friend Hayden Floyd, also from Duford. He died in combat in eastern France four days earlier.

Private First Class Fletcher "Bud" Blanton must have joined Company D in late November as it took up its position inside the German border near Aachen. We know from the account of his chaplain and of a new friend he made in the company that he was an easy soldier to get to know and to like—a noticeable detail because replacements were not immediately befriended by most longtime unit members. That distance from the new soldiers made the loss less hurtful for the rest of the unit when a replacement was killed. But the young soldier with the bright eyes and soft-spoken down-home manner, the one who talked all the time about his mother and sisters and little hamlets like Nichols and Duford, made friends quickly. In appearance he was still a fuzzy-cheeked boy and was almost immediately accepted throughout Company D.

He mailed a sobering letter to his mother December 7, 1944, announcing his company was on the front line.

> I am about to realize what the war is all about. I wish part of the men back home could see how it is over here. I bet they would go an get under the bed at home an stay there until after the war is over instead of going out and having a different movie ever night. I often think about how lucky some of the people back home are an about how foolish I used to do when I was back home. I used to go

out with some girl and spend all of the money you had or most of it. That was about a year ago. An about 3 or 4 times a week I would get high. I never did get enough sleep. Instead of doing that now I go to bed when I get a chance an pray that this war will be over soon instead of thinking about where I would go the next night. This is a crazy time to think about something like that but it is all true. Mom I wont get very much money a month but I am going to send it home so I will have a little when I get back.

In the same letter he warned his mother:

Some of the boys heard from home an their mothers had a message that they were wounded in action. But they were as well as ever. So if you ever hear that I am wounded or anything is wrong think nothing of it for they get things mixed up over hear. I hope I never get in battle but if I do I will trust in the Lord and do my best.

A day later he wrote his mother that he wanted to take care of her and the family when he got home.

I am going to send a little home ever month. If it is not more than $10.00 or $15.00 it will help a little. If I was to send $15.00 a month and the $10.00 bond I have out that would be $25.00 ever month. And if this war lasts as long as I think it will I will have a good little sum of money. And I sure will need it after I get home. I want to run a store after the war. I never dont want a lot of money. I just want enough for me and you Son and Ralph to live good on. For I no Betty and Bessie will be married when I get back.

He wrote his sister Clarise, my mother, on December 14:

The ground froze this morning. Just think its only 11 more days until Christmas. I wish I was home. I sure would like to see Santa Clause. I wonder if there is a Santa Clause in Germany. I bet Santa come over here to get his apples for Christmas. There is so many apples over here. If you see Santa tell him if he has anything for me save it until next Christmas an I might get it then for I will be their. I have some beechnut chewing gum now an I had some mounds candy bars one day this week. I havent been paid since I came across. The government must think I am working for nothing. I couldn't spend my money if I had it so I am satisfied if they dont pay me until I get back to the states I guess. I had better sign off for this time. So keep sweet and write me often. Lots of Love an Luck Bud

The Germans launched the Ardennes Offensive December 16, 1944, and this attack to the south of the division's position within Germany put most of the US battle plans on hold until the offensive could be thwarted. Two days later he wrote again:

I am getting along fine. I guess you think all I write is about something to eat. Well I am eating mixed nuts now an boy are they good. I haven't gotten any mail yet. I am just waiting and hoping. I have some clean clothes on one more time. I have written ever one in the family now an I am not going to write very much until I hear from home for I dont no anything to write. Write soon an keep sweet.
Lots of Love an Luck BUD

His next letter was written Christmas night:

Dearest Mama,
I wonder what you are doing tonight. I am fine I guess. I have had a nice Christmas dinner an some hershey candy. I hope you are all fine. I haven't got any mail yet. I am still hoping to get some soon. I am a messenger now. I sure am glad I was changed. My Sargent is from N.C. and is a good Sargent. Tell everbody Hello an write soon. I haven't written for about five days now but I write ever chance I get. Tell Ralph an Son Hello.
Lots of Love Bud

He continued to write regularly and posted three letters December 28, one headed with the added note, "Three Oclock At Night." He wrote:

Mama I pray to God ever night that he will carry me through this war safe and get me home to you and the rest of the family. I also pray for you and everbody back in the states an for the ones over here. Its strange that I had never thought of God before as I do now. But I have asked for his help an deep down in my heart I no he has answered my prayers. Mama keep sweet until I get back and tell everbody hello. I am going to write Son and Ralph a letter now. Lots of Love an Luck BUD

On December 31, he wrote:

I am getting anything to eat that I want now but I have to cook it. It is all canned food. All that has to be done is to just warm it good. We get lots of jelly an butter cream an coffee.

By this time most of his company had moved into German homes near and in Mariaweiler outside Düren, Germany.

He wrote again two days later:

Mama I dont have time to write a long letter now. I just wanted to write a few lines to let you no that I was well an getting plenty to eat an a warm place to sleep so you wouldn't worry an imagine I was sleeping in a fox hole. Tell everbody hello an to be good. Write when you can.
Lots of Love an Luck BUD

Even as his mail delayed by the Atlantic crossing finally caught up with him on January 5, 1945, he still wanted more. He wrote:

I got 3 from Dot, 1 from Clarise 1 from Bessie 1 from Betty but I didn't hear from you. I hope to hear from you today. Tell them I will answer their letters as soon as I can. The letter was mailed the 1 of Nov. An I got it the 4 of Jan. All most two month since it was mailed.

On January 7 he wrote:

Mama you could never realize how much getting mail can build up my morale. I believe the boys over here would go crazy if they didn't get mail once in a while. Mama I got a letter today an I opened it to read it an it started off (Dearest Darling) an soon as I look at that I decided that it wasn't my mail. But I look on the envelope an it was still mine. I feel big somebody calling me Dearest Darling. Of course it didn't make me mad.

Private First Class Fletcher Stanley Blanton was up before day on the morning of January 10, 1945, and at his post as messenger at company headquarters before daybreak. A few minutes after 5 AM a German artillery barrage rained down around the command building. When the medics cleared the rubble, they found his shattered body. He had been killed instantly.

CHAPTER 3

The First Year Without Him

Norton (Marvin B. Norton) and myself were scouts and leading
the platoon across an open field munching on some raw turnips.
As we had gone along for awhile, I said to Norton, "Hell, I haven't
seen a German yet, this might not be so bad after all." Then we hear
a machine gun and notice that the ground is kicking up around us.
Norton says, "Holy hell, they're shooting at us," and we headed back
like a bat out of hell for a barn close by, looking for cover. Some
scouts, eh? I remember that same day being alongside Jesus Polanco
(Pfc Jesus F. Polanco, KIA 25 Oct 44) when he was hit and killed and
I knew then that this was not a lark or a game but a dreadful reality
that maybe I would not see my Dad again.

—*Edward L. Ritzer, Company B, 414th Infantry Regiment*

In retrospect, I probably could have done many things differently
than I did, which might have saved someone's life, but I did the
best that I could at the time. To paraphrase someone, "my combat
experiences were the greatest adventures of my life. I wouldn't take a
million for them, and wouldn't give two cents to repeat them."

—*Robert E. Woods, Company E, 414th Infantry Regiment*

Holland-south of Zundert (65) (25–26 Oct) Walked smack into 3
Heinie machine guns here. Ambush. Pitch black nite. Men too close
together. 2nd Battalion pinned down in columns of 4. Bullets hitting
ground all around us. 36 killed. Most complete disorganization in

all our combat operations. Everyone on their own. Closest to death here. Unbelievable, but 1 or 2 men were so tired they fell asleep and snored between enemy machine gun firings. Retreat orderly. Germans used flares, grenades, mortars and small arms. Sgt. Allen tried to get mortar group to return fire. Next morning, men saw the bullet holes thru their backpacks, canteens and mess kits.

—*Frank J. Perozzi, Company F, 414th Infantry Regiment*

Nichols Railway Depot manager Clarence Leslie Willis was a popular man with Bud Blanton's brothers Carol and Ralph. Only a couple of years before, they had been promised a red wagon for Christmas by their mother. "My brothers had searched the house all day and couldn't find that wagon momma had promised them," Betty Blanton Mincey recalled. "But it arrived at the train depot and Mr. Willis delivered it late on Christmas Eve. The boys didn't see Mr. Willis come by and when they found that wagon under the tree, they said they were convinced once and for all that there really was a Santa Claus."

But the same Clarence Willis brought no joy in mid-January 1945. He handed my grandmother a Western Union telegraph envelope. It was a duty he had performed several times before in the past two years, and he knew the words contained inside by heart, as did practically all station agents in World War II. The message that day stated, "THE ARMY DEEPLY REGRETS THAT YOUR SON FLETCHER BLANTON PRIVATE FIRST CLASS WAS KILLED IN ACTION IN THE PERFORMANCE OF HIS DUTY AND IN THE SERVICE OF HIS COUNTRY." There were no details on how or when or where Bud Blanton was killed.

Jessie Mae Blanton read the telegram and went to bed immediately. "Momma couldn't handle it," Betty Mincey said. "Naturally, I remember that we were all hush, hush. Everybody was upset. Sally, Son and Ralph and I were in the house. All the neighbors responded. That's how Nichols is. People came by bringing casseroles and flowers. The Gilmores and the Battles, families we knew. Virginia Battle was living in Nichols and she came. The Connellys came over from next door. Worth Norman came too. We lived right behind the Normans. He ran the local garage and Clarise worked in the office there for him. Everybody was good to momma."[1]

In the days that followed, Bud Blanton's letters continued to come to the Blanton mailbox one after another, and knowing my grandmother I can imagine the grief she endured as she lived the final days and hours of her son's life through his own words. In his final letter dated January 9, 1945, received long after the notice of his death, he wrote:

Dearest Mama

How are you getting along these cold winter days. I hope you are all fine. I am fine only I have a cold but it isn't very bad. I hope Ralph is getting along fine with his broken leg.

I didn't get any mail today or yesterday but I got enough Sunday to last a few days. I hope you have been getting my mail. I write you ever day. I have been having plenty time lately to write. It has been snowing for the past two days. The snow is about a foot deep now. Mom I am getting along fine. I get plenty to eat and have a warm place to sleep ever night. The time sure pass fast over here. I sure will be glad when the Jerrys surrender. I guess that will be the happiest time of all our life. Son told me in his letter that Roosevelt won the election. I am sending a $35.00 money order home. If you need it use it. I will write again when I can. Write soon and keep sweet and tell ever body hello.

Lots of Love and Luck

Bud

The same night he also wrote his sister Clarise, my mother:

I guess you are surprised to hear from me. I hope you have been getting my mail. I have been writing you all often. I try to write ever chance I get. I don't want you all to think its rough over here for its not. I am getting plenty to eat an have a warm place to sleep. Bye the way I got a shower an some clean clothes last week. I want you to see if you can't stop this war. I believe the germans are about ready to quit fighting anyway. I no we sure are. I am not mad with any body an I don't think its nice to kill. So the sooner this war stops the better it will be for all of us. Some of the boys don't write home often. I guess they have their folks thinking they dont have time that they are fighting to hard. I have just gotten through writing mama, and I sent her a money order for $35.00. I guess I better close and write Dot. I have been

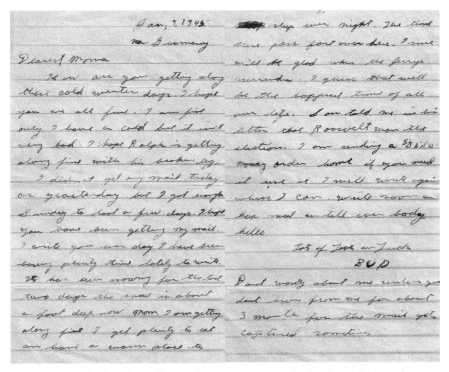

Figure 8. The last letter home, January 9, 1945. Collection of the author.

getting mail pretty often. I wrote Will one day. I hope I hear from him soon.
Excuse this paper. My German stationery is given out.
Lots of Love and Luck
Bud

We know now the letters had been written somewhere in Mariaweiler, Germany, on the outskirts of Düren, where his company and the Timberwolf Division had fought its way to the banks of the Roer River, fifteen miles east of Aachen. From his earlier letters, it is safe to assume that he wrote his last letter from one of the buildings commandeered by the soldiers as they took the town. Most likely he and his squad members cooked their own evening meal and then he sat down to write a letter to his mother as was his daily habit. As noted, he also wrote one to his sister Clarise and most certainly one to Dot Floyd. He had written earlier that his habit, since moving indoors, was to sleep in a bed in his uniform. He got up before day and we can be fairly sure he strapped on his gear, shouldered his M-1 Garand .30–06 rifle, and walked through the foot-deep snow to the Company D, 413th Infantry command building. There he took his post as company messenger. He had been recently promoted to messenger, or company runner as his fellow soldiers called it. Earlier, his family had been told, he had trained and served as a machine gun loader, one of the most dangerous jobs in combat. At 5:20 AM, the command building was hit by artillery fire and the men scrambled for cover. Bud Blanton was not among them. He had been fatally wounded. From his birth in the back bedroom of the Blanton farmhouse until he took his post that morning, he had lived 20 years and 45 days.

Jessie Mae Blanton wanted to know the final details of her son's life and his death. It is much the same for every family. Amidst the sorrow there is almost always a need to know about those last moments. And in World War II the process of that discovery was painfully slow.

Even as the letters Bud Blanton had written to his mother and Dot and his brothers and sisters continued to arrive in Nichols, the Army and War Department began sending the documents and formal declarations and expressions of sympathy that followed the death of a service member. The January 31 notice of the posthumous award of the Purple Heart was delivered by mail in early February. The letter from the War Department was signed by Major General J. A. Ulio, the Army Adjutant General. A few days later the actual medal arrived at the Blanton home, sent by Brigadier General Roland Walsh from the Army Quartermaster Depot in Philadelphia. Secretary of War Henry Stimson wrote to confirm awarding of the medal: "The loss of a loved one is beyond man's repairing, and the medal is of slight value; not so, however, the message it carries. We are all comrades in arms in this battle for our country, and those who have gone are not, and never will be, forgotten by those of us who remain. I hope you will accept the medal in evidence of such remembrance."

South Carolina Governor Ransome J. Williams wrote my grandmother: "The sacrifice that your loved one has made will be long remembered in the hearts of his fellow South Carolinians."

Army Chief of Staff General George Marshall sent a card, one delivered only to Gold Star families who had lost a loved one in the war. He

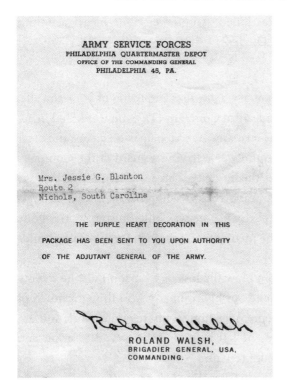

ARMY SERVICE FORCES
PHILADELPHIA QUARTERMASTER DEPOT
OFFICE OF THE COMMANDING GENERAL
PHILADELPHIA 45, PA.

Mrs. Jessie G. Blanton
Route 2
Nichols, South Carolina

THE PURPLE HEART DECORATION IN THIS
PACKAGE HAS BEEN SENT TO YOU UPON AUTHORITY
OF THE ADJUTANT GENERAL OF THE ARMY.

ROLAND WALSH,
BRIGADIER GENERAL, USA,
COMMANDING.

Figure 9. Purple Heart Award letter sent to Jessie Blanton. Collection of the author.

told my grandmother: "Your son fought valiantly in a supreme hour of his country's need. His memory will live in the grateful heart of our nation."

Sympathy cards and letters poured in from friends and family. Many of them were at the bottom of the bag I found in the garage attic seventy-seven years after his death. One of the cards in the box was from the Blantons' neighbor Janice Gilmore, wife of the Nichols doctor, Harold Gilmore. The couple lived around the corner from the Blantons. Janice Gilmore chose a card with a poem from James Whitcomb Riley who wrote, "I cannot say, and I will not say that he is dead—he is just away!" Janice Gilmore understood more than others the sense of loss my grandmother felt. Mrs. Gilmore's parents, Edward and Vera Buchan Harbort, were missionaries in the Philippines taken prisoner by the Japanese in June 1942. Fortunately for Janice Gilmore, the Harborts were freed a month after my uncle's death.

My grandmother told her children she appreciated the cards and the awards for her son. But she wanted to know how he died. And on January 25, 1945, with help from her daughter Clarise, she wrote the Army inquiring how Bud Blanton was killed. An answer came nearly a month later from Chaplain Edward P. Doyle:

Dear Mrs. Blanton:

I have received your letter of January 25th, 1945 inquiring of your son Pfc. Fletcher Blanton, 34865007, formerly of Company "D," who was killed in action the 10th of January 1945 in Germany. At 5:20 o'clock on a cool and clear morning, January 10th Pfc. Blanton was relieving a guard at the Company Command Post. While doing so, the immediate area was struck by a barrage of enemy artillery fire. Fletcher was struck by shrapnel from this barrage. There was no suffering on his part since he was killed instantly. His body was cared for immediately by the medics who occupied the adjoining building.

I can well understand what a blow the loss of your son must be to you. Fletcher is missed by many friends of his company who thought much of him. May I assure you that I remember him in my religious work and am not unmindful of the dear ones he left behind. Asking God to grant you strength and courage in this trial, I remain

Sincerely yours, Fr. Edward P. Doyle Chaplain, AUS[2]

In the months after Bud's death, Jessie Mae Blanton shielded the younger children from awareness of her difficult financial situation. There was almost no money coming in. My uncle had sent home war bonds for her to use, but the local bank would not cash them without his signature.

Her financial hardship was clear from the correspondence received from various Army representatives. The family was to receive Bud Blanton's $10,000 serviceman's life insurance policy, and Mrs. Blanton was entitled to a pension. But the wheels of the bureaucracy moved slowly. More than three months after my uncle's death, on April 14, 1945, 1st Lieutenant Ruth McClain at Fort Moultrie, South Carolina, wrote:

We are indeed sorry that you find yourself in financial difficulty at this time. Because of the volume of work handled by the Veterans Administration, it is difficult to judge the time involved in processing a claim. However, if you hear nothing concerning your pension claim in the near future, contact this office again and we will attempt to trace it for you.

I assume that you have received the check for the 6 months' gratuity pay. This check is intended to cover the period of time until you start receiving other benefits such as insurance and pension. However, if you find you cannot make ends meet until such payments begin, you should contact your local Red Cross chapter who is authorized to give you financial assistance during that period.

If this office can be of further assistance do not hesitate to contact us.

With his service in combat and other qualifications Bud Blanton earned about $70 per month. And the initial gratuity paycheck sent to his mother amounted to approximately $400.

Throughout the years of the Great Depression in the 1930s, Fletcher and Jessie Blanton and their children had lived a life of rural poverty known by hundreds of thousands of American farm families. They had food to eat because they grew vegetables. And occasionally they could slaughter a hog, salt the meat, and feed the family. The Blanton sons, when old enough, hunted the nearby woods on and around the farm for squirrels, rabbits, and deer to supplement the food supply. There was no money for luxuries. The little income received from my grandfather Fletcher's share of the sale of the tobacco crop was barely enough to buy salt, sugar, flour, and the other essentials at the general store. Clothing was often hand-me-downs and whatever my grandmother could sew.

A 1937 Horry County Tax Receipt found in the bag that contained my uncle's letters showed that the value of all the personal property Fletcher and Jessie Mae Blanton possessed after twenty-two years of marriage was $255. That year they paid state, county, and school taxes totaling $16.07 and a $3 road tax.

As noted above, the local bank refused to cash the war bonds Bud Blanton sent his mother; it required a death certificate in addition to the telegram from the War Department. Apparently, the additional documentation from the Army would not suffice. My grandmother asked her daughter Clarise (my mother) to solve the problem. And Clarise Blanton Walker's draft letter from 1945, also preserved in the bag of letters and photos, shows the difficulty the family encountered. She wrote the Bureau of Vital Statistics at the state capital in Columbia shortly after her brother's death. After two months with no answer, she tried again:

> I wrote your office about two months ago asking for information as to how I could secure a death certificate for my brother Fletcher Blanton 34865007, of the 413th Infantry Regiment Company D who was killed in Germany Jan. 10, 1945. I have not received an answer and I do not know anywhere else that I could secure this death certificate. Please send me the proper place to apply if you cannot forward this information. Also the cost and I will send proper remittance.

In June the Army asked if the family would like to receive my uncle's personal effects, warning that the items were bloodstained. His property, the Army reported, amounted to $2.25 in US currency, some souvenir German marks, a pocketknife, photographs, and his South Carolina driver's license. Clarise, writing for her mother, said that the family wanted all his personal items despite the bloodstains.

That summer, a man about Bud Blanton's age and size with eyes and a look that seemed sad and strangely old for someone that young, knocked at Jessie Mae Blanton's front door. The young man introduced himself as Willie Bishop from Taylors, South Carolina, near Greenville. He explained that he had been in Company D with Bud and was with him at Mariaweiler those last days. The two had made a pact, he said. If one survived and the other did not, the one who came home would visit the family of the other.

Willie Bishop could not tell the Blantons exactly how Bud had died. The soldiers in the company disagreed on that, he told them. One had talked about a sniper and said Bud had been hit standing in a doorway. Willie was not certain and the Blantons did have Chaplain Doyle's report. No matter how it happened, my grandmother knew it would not bring her son back alive. What she did have was the presence of a young man who had known Bud up until the last hours of his life.

Almost instantly, the Blantons decided Willie Bishop would become a family member. The knock at the door, the first meeting, and the story of my uncle's life and death in Germany became a part of family lore and Willie Bishop found himself in a lifelong friendship—no, an adopted kinship, with Bud Blanton's family, his mother, his siblings, even the children of his

Figure 10. Blanton family visits Willie Bishop's home, ca. 1950.
Left to right: Jessie, Vera, Ralph, Clarise, Betty, Sally, and Son.
Photo from collection of the author.

friend's siblings. The relationship stretched across sixty years until Willie Bishop's death in 2007.

I can close my eyes and remember the excitement in my mother's voice saying, "Willie Bishop is coming. He was Bud's friend. You have to meet him." And my father, who was extremely selective in his choice of friends, revered Willie as a war hero like his brother-in-law Bud. My Aunt Betty reported on every visit with Willie Bishop and kept up with all the details of his life for the next half century.

The Blanton family members rarely left the Pee Dee, but when they did it was often to visit the Bishop family at Taylors. Immediately after the war, Willie lived in one of those clapboard-sided company mill houses common to the upstate. I recall my first visit when I was 5 or 6. There, in Taylors, we found the mantel in the Bishop home lined with golf trophies. Willie's son William "Steve" Bishop was already an outstanding junior golfer. He later became a touring pro and eventually a club pro in Florida.

*Figure 11. Fletcher's brothers Ralph (left) and Son (right) with
Willie Bishop (center). Jack Belcher is on the far right.
Collection of the author.*

Through it all, Willie Bishop remained true to his vow to stay in touch with his friend Bud's family until the end of his life.[3]

Later that year a young man named Jack Belcher also came to the Blanton house with Willie Bishop. He, too, was in Bud's unit and they had exchanged the same promise to visit if the other did not survive. Unlike the contact with Willie Bishop, my family lost touch with Jack Belcher after half a dozen years. And a third soldier eventually stopped by. He had made the same agreement with Bud.

"I just can't remember the name of the third boy," Betty Mincey said. "It has been a very long time. I know that there were three of them and that Momma corresponded with them. They were real loyal to her. But Willie was the one who kept coming back."

In August 1945, my grandmother received a letter from a woman in Landrum, South Carolina:

Dear Mrs. Blanton,

My son has returned from Germany, he was in the 413 Inf, 104th Div, he told me of a boy named Fletcher Blanton, a platoon runner that was killed while he was on guard duty, he was killed instantly by a mortar shell. He & another boy was standing in the doorway at the commanding post. The other boy was not hurt. At the time of the accident they were stationed in Rhur Valley near Duren. I thought that you would like to know about his death from some one that was with him at the time. They were in the same platoon.

I was not sure about the name being Fletcher but thought that was right, said he always talked about his mother & sister said his father was dead. and he remembered that he was from Nichols, South Carolina So I hope you get this information. I have a neighbor who lost her youngest son, she worried so much wondering just how he was killed. So a few days ago she received a letter from his Sgt. telling her just how he was killed, and she said she could feel better knowing he did not have to suffer long. So if you have never heard before about your son, I hope this will help you. So sorry he could not come back.

My son is on his way to Calif. Left Thursday, hope this war is going to be over soon, have listened all day hoping to hear it is over.

If any one else get this letter please give it to Fletcher's mother.

Mrs. J. H. Atkins
Landrum, South Carolina

At Christmas that year, Mrs. Atkins sent a card. She wrote:

Wish you could come to Landrum to see me. Would like to know you better. If I ever have a chance I am coming to see you.

Mrs. J. H. Atkins

The two women never met in person.

Nora Culbreth Atkins (Mrs. J. H.) died in 1984 at the age of 89, thirty-one years after her husband's death. Their son, William Cecil Atkins, who was a member of Company D with my uncle, died in 1976 at the age of 56.

The Blanton family finally solved the problem of cashing my uncle's war bonds, and the government life insurance policy payment was settled during the course of the year. My grandmother chose to take the $10,000 in $50 monthly increments. She continued sewing for townspeople. Her sons Ralph (9) and Son (12) and daughter Sally (17) still lived in the family home. Daughter Clarise was a few blocks away in an apartment at the Nichols Hotel with her husband Will and their 6-month-old son. C. P. Mincey returned from duty in the Pacific Theater, and he and Betty eventually found a home down the street, a log cabin without running water. Edna Blanton Scott lived nearby with her husband Hubert, the Nichols Chief of Police. Vera and John E. Elvington were in Fayetteville, North Carolina, where he ran a Woolworth Five and Dime store.[4]

The war ended with the formal surrender of the Japanese on September 2, 1945, and over the coming months the family sought to resume a normal life. "Everyone tried to get back to their lives," Betty Mincey recalled. But her deeply religious mother was not at peace. Her son was not with them. She wanted him home to say a final goodbye and to bury him in the good soil of Horry County where she could visit any time she wished.

It would take two more years for her prayers to be answered.

CHAPTER 4

Coming Home

The entrance to the house was a door at street level right on the main street. We agreed that I would open the door, throw in a grenade, shut the door and then yank it open as soon as the grenade went off. My partner would then leap through the door and catch any remaining Germans by surprise. We proceeded according to plan. After the grenade exploded, my partner hurled himself through the door with his M-1 ready to fire. Unfortunately the door opened onto a basement stairway entry and the grenade explosion had apparently blown the stairway down. In any event the stairway ended up in a pile on the basement floor and my partner ended up down there on top of it. Getting him out of the basement took a lot longer than any of our other tasks that day. He was uninjured despite the drop of some ten feet or more. A tribute to his training or his youth.

—*Gerald Waterman, Company A, 415th Infantry Regiment*

The big excitement came on a beautiful sunny day when we crossed the Rhine at Remagen. The 104th was among the early troops to make the crossing. Americans on the far side of the Rhine! This was the beginning of the end for the Third Reich. Unfortunately our battery was directed into an area full of German mines. Here Amos Bartz, our senior F.O. (forward observer), who had escaped so many dangerous moments got his purple heart. We all carried morphine and I was able to give Amos and several others their morphine shots. I think it helped. It was a mess. We lost a couple of good men, but fortunately there were no German planes to strafe us, so we got out with just minimum casualties.

—*Carl Livingston, Jr., Battery A, 366th Field Artillery*

We shortly resumed our offensive dash northwestward toward Lippstadt, where Combat Command A linked up with elements of the 9th U.S. Army at about 1400 hours that Easter Sunday (April 1, 1945), completing the encirclement of some 350,000 German troops.

We billeted in Lippstadt that night, in a house containing several young German females. They were soon joined by several others who requested permission to remain with us because they were frightened. I recall the girls singing Lili Marlene for our entertainment as we, without concern, again violated the U.S. Army non-fraternization policy. The following day we resumed our eastward advance through badly burned-out Paderborn toward the Weser River.

—*Eiler Ravnholt, Company D, 414th Infantry Regiment*

Private First Class Fletcher Blanton came home from World War II on Thursday, November 4, 1948. The Timberwolf Division combat infantryman's casket, accompanied by military escort, arrived in Mullins on the Seaboard Airline Railroad train in late morning after the five-hour trip from Charlotte, North Carolina. Charles Mackey Jr., manager of Meares Funeral Home in Mullins, met the train and the casket was driven three blocks down South Main St. to the Meares building. It was the same funeral home to which Bud's father Fletcher had been taken after his death in 1940.

"That night and the next we had flowers in momma's living room and a picture of Bud beside the flowers," his sister Betty Mincey recalled. The night before the funeral there was a knock at the door, she said.

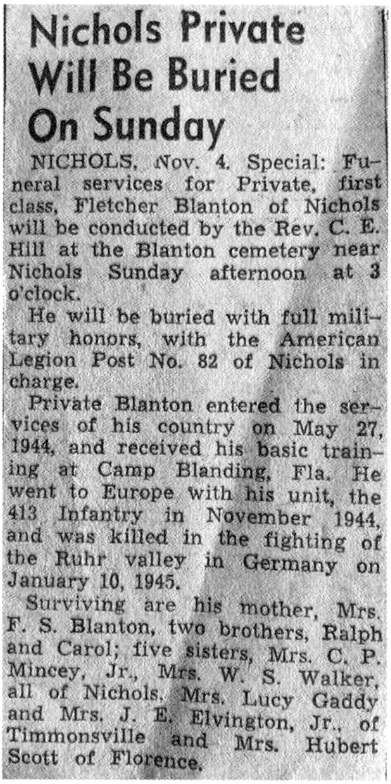

Nichols Private Will Be Buried On Sunday

NICHOLS, Nov. 4. Special: Funeral services for Private, first class, Fletcher Blanton of Nichols will be conducted by the Rev. C. E. Hill at the Blanton cemetery near Nichols Sunday afternoon at 3 o'clock.

He will be buried with full military honors, with the American Legion Post No. 82 of Nichols in charge.

Private Blanton entered the services of his country on May 27, 1944, and received his basic training at Camp Blanding, Fla. He went to Europe with his unit, the 413 Infantry in November 1944, and was killed in the fighting of the Ruhr valley in Germany on January 10, 1945.

Surviving are his mother, Mrs. F. S. Blanton, two brothers, Ralph and Carol; five sisters, Mrs. C. P. Mincey, Jr., Mrs. W. S. Walker, all of Nichols, Mrs. Lucy Gaddy and Mrs. J. E. Elvington, Jr., of Timmonsville and Mrs. Hubert Scott of Florence.

Figure 12. Fletcher "Bud" Blanton's reinterment announcement in 1948. Florence Morning News. The reinterment was overseen by American Legion Post No. 82. From collection of the author.

Willie Bishop and Jack Belcher and the other boy whose name I cannot remember came to the house. They had all been with Bud in combat. Momma was so surprised to see them. They said they could not sleep. They said that Bud had been the youngest in their company and they had always looked after him. They said they had made a promise to him and they wanted to sit up with him that night even though the body was at the funeral home and not there.

The previous day the largest area newspaper, the *Florence Morning News,* had run a story with the headline FALLEN NICHOLS VETERAN HOME. The article noted: "Funeral Services for Private First Class Fletcher Blanton of Nichols will be conducted by the Rev. C. E. Hill at the Blanton cemetery Sunday afternoon at 3 o'clock."[1]

The year 1948 was a time when America's war dead were being brought home from overseas in large numbers as families were given the option of letting their loved ones remain in military cemeteries abroad or reburying them in the US. In that year a hearse bearing an American flag-draped coffin was a familiar sight all over the country.

On Sunday afternoon, November 7, a line of cars with headlights lit followed the black Meares hearse out of Mullins. The weather was unusually warm for early November, reaching 70 degrees as the procession made its way on US Highway 76 along the seven miles of blacktop to Nichols, then swung around the sharp curve in the middle of town and passed East Raft Street on the left. Many in the long line of cars would have known that the Blanton home was only four hundred feet away down East Raft where it joined Averette Street, the dusty dirt track that served as the backstreet of Nichols.

Eight miles further, at the Blanton cemetery, the honor guard of the newly organized Nichols American Legion Post 82 came to attention when the procession arrived. The Post members included C. P. Mincey and Will Walker, brothers-in-law of Bud Blanton.[2]

The funeral service was attended by dozens of Nichols residents and nearly all the Blanton family members. Bud's mother and his brothers, Carol and Ralph, were there along with his sisters, Betty Mincey and Clarise Walker of Nichols, Sally Gaddy and Vera Elvington of Timmonsville, and Edna Scott of Florence.

"You were there too," my Aunt Betty said to me when I asked about the service by Reverend Charlie Hill. "You were three years old," she said. "And my daughter Cindy, who was one, was there also."

Nichols American Legion Post 82 rendered military honors and the final salutes were led by three former Timberwolf Division soldiers unfamiliar to most who attended. Willie Bishop and Jack Belcher and the wartime friend whose name my family members can no longer recall knew Bud Blanton in a way those who have not gone to war can never understand. They had once been four vital, young infantrymen fighting for their country. But now the youngest of them, the fuzzy-cheeked farm boy, who loved to talk about his mother and his sisters and brothers and his home in South Carolina, was at the end of his journey while theirs continued. Such was love and luck and fate.

CHAPTER 5

Those He Left Behind

The 104th Timberwolf Division had seen much action by the time
we arrived at Nordhausen, but no one knew of the existence of concentration camps. When we walked through those gates, we could
see that the buildings had been bombed, roofs were half gone, and
rubble was all over the place. But what startled us and made us think
we were in Hell were the stacks of bodies! Some stacks were three
and four people high, some nude and some in tattered garments.
Even hardened soldiers looked about them in bewilderment at this
terrible scene.

In a corner three men huddled about a low fire, and next to them
was the head of a decayed and rotting horse which evidently they
used for food. Maggots and flies were also making a meal from these
leftovers and more than one person gagged as they saw and smelled
the repugnant horror.

Each medical corpsman was assigned a building to check.
Inside, bedracks were stacked one on top of the other and living
were together with the dead, too weak to crawl away. Those alive
could barely speak, their eyes were shrunken in their heads, bones
protruded from matchstick thin arms and legs, and only a groan or
whimper made us realize that they were still alive.

The officer in charge commandeered some Germans to empty
homes and three blocks of buildings were evacuated as we started
moving the living-dead into them. As some were pleading for water,
we gave them some, only to realize that sometimes they could die or

get very ill from that! In their starved condition, we could only give them very small sips, or feed them intravenously.

Later we were told that this camp held not only Jews but political prisoners, as well as an American airman that had been shot down. These people had been used for forced labor at the V-2 rocket assembly plants and had been given a loaf of bread a week for six men!

Even the Chaplain—who I had never heard say a curse word during all our days of battle—cursed those responsible for this unbelievable cruelty.

To get back to our going thru bunks. As I walked through, I saw a man with a "J" on his uniform and spoke to him in Yiddish since I presumed he was Jewish. This man fell to his knees crying, and kissing my hands. I always get so emotional when I talk of this "Joe Gelber." There but for the Grace of God would I be as a Jew!

I gave Joe all my rations and took his picture and promised to give it to his Aunt, as he told me he had a relative in the Bronx.

As we moved people into the homes that had been made available, we did what best we could to keep them alive. But even as we gave them small sips of liquid, some would die.

The 104th had to move out after two days. This was towards the end of the War, and shortly after I returned to the United States I found the picture of Joe Gelber in my knapsack and went to the Bronx to give it to Joe's aunt. When we arrived there was a man in the house . . . and it was Joe! His aunt on learning that he was alive, had sent for him and his wife, who had miraculously survived by working as a seamstress in a work camp. I hardly recognized him as of course he had gained back his weight. It was a joyous reunion.

—*Seymour Zipper, 329th Medical Battalion, 104th Infantry Division*

I have spent a lifetime watching the brothers and sisters of Bud Blanton live and, sadly in recent years, also die. I know about each of them, my aunts and uncles, from personal experience. But until the letters appeared, I knew little about Bud Blanton. He was only a picture on a wall and a loving memory formed mostly from conversations with my mother and my Aunt Betty. That changed dramatically when I found his letters. Now I consider myself, along with my cousin Charles Fletcher Mincey, next in the family line to keep the memory of his service to country alive. And that extends also to the memory of the other servicemen whose names turned up in the research for this book.

In hundreds of thousands of homes in our country there is a special picture on the mantle or hanging in a prominent place in the living room. That picture is a reminder of a serviceman or woman who made the ultimate sacrifice for country. As a US Army veteran, I am the current commander of Nichols American Legion Post 82, the same post that rendered honors at Bud Blanton's reinterment in 1948. The Legion was there for Bud Blanton's family in the same way it strives to be there today for all veterans and their families.

About 16 million Americans served in World War II, but in early 2023 there were only about 167,000 of them alive. Our World War II veterans leave us at the rate of nearly 180 per day. My Uncle C. P. Mincey is the last remaining World War II veteran in the family and in our Legion post. He is 97.

Bud Blanton's letters home also caused me to reflect on the lives of the family members and friends he left behind. In a way the lives they were able to lead after the war mirrored many elements of what he might have experienced had he survived. I also considered what the relationships might have been had he returned from the war. In brief, here is what happened to his family and friends and my thoughts on how things might have been for him in the postwar world.

JESSIE MAE GRAHAM BLANTON

Bud's mother Jessie Mae Blanton lived nearly eighteen years after her son's death. Born in 1899, her life spanned World War I, the Roaring Twenties, the Great Depression, World War II, and the Korean War. After her son died in the war, she watched as her remaining seven children grew safely to adulthood and established meaningful lives for themselves. All married and all but two had children. She moved from the rented house on the

Figure 13. The Blanton cemetery near Duford
crossroads in Horry County. Photo by the author.

back street to a nicer rental home at the east end of Nichols a few years after her son's reinterment. In 1955, when her daughter Betty and husband C. P. Mincey moved to a farm outside town from their home on Raft Street, she moved to their house in town.

Jessie Blanton was close to her children and in some ways even closer to her grandchildren. She took great pleasure in having the family in her home for Sunday meals. Her children knew the sacrifices she had made to raise and support them. Her two remaining sons were the last to leave home, and both revered their mother. She built, by sterling example, a strong family unit exhibiting determination, hard work, and a love that surmounted many heartaches over the sixty-plus years of her life.

"When I think of what she faced with the loss of her husband in 1940 and the fact she had eight children, five of them still at home, I know she was a great woman," said C. P. Mincey.

As a grandson I am admittedly prejudiced in my judgment, but I think her the finest, most caring grandmother anyone could wish. She died

Figure 14. The Blanton sisters. Left to right: Edna, Clarise, Vera, Sally, and Betty. Personal collection of the author.

December 20, 1963, at Mullins Hospital of a coronary occlusion and was buried in the Blanton cemetery near her eldest son.

VERA

Vera Marie Blanton, born 1916, was the oldest child. Her sister Betty said Vera should have been a boy; she spent a lot of time following her father around like a young boy. My Uncle Bud called her Boo because she could be gruff, downright scary, and intimidating. There is a family picture that shows the five Blanton girls as adults and seems to reflect the personality each one took on as a married woman. In the photograph, my Aunt Edna is on the left looking competent but highly restrained; my mother Clarise, next, appears open, friendly, and vulnerable. On the right Betty looks efficient and capable. Sally, next to her, radiates confidence and athletic bearing with a hint of mischievousness. Vera, in the middle, appears haughty with her head raised to the left and eyes nearly closed, tolerating the photographer, and the world, for a brief moment.

Vera married John E. Elvington in 1941. They had no children and spent their lives running convenience stores in North and South Carolina. For all her bluster, my Aunt Vera was kind to her nieces and nephews. But she and John E. were all about work. For many years they ran a 7–Eleven convenience food and beverage store on Rosewood Drive in Columbia and spent practically every waking hour in that store. Later they moved to Timmonsville where they ran a corner store. To me their lives always seemed unfulfilled. Over the years I saw only a few brief flashes of real joy in her face. I can't say that I ever saw John E. appear happy. My aunt never gave me any reason to think her lot in life was anything but good. However, I am certain that Bud Blanton, who wrote about his ambition to own a store when he came home, would not have wanted the life Vera and John E. chose. And after being on the front lines, he would not have been intimidated by Aunt Boo. But he would have admired her pluck.

Vera died in 1982 and John E. in 1983. They are buried at Riverside Cemetery in Horry County.

EDNA

Edna Earl Blanton, born 1919, married Hubert Scott in 1943. He was a police officer, first in Nichols and later in Florence. Like her mother, Edna was a seamstress. She and Hubert had no children. Hubert's primary goal in life seemed to be pinching pennies and accumulating a million dollars in the bank by the time he reached retirement age. Edna was loving. On occasion she could laugh, a sort of abbreviated, nervous laugh, as if she were permitted only brief moments of joy. She was soft spoken, unassuming, and yet always on edge. She died in 2003 and Hubert in 2017. Before his death in a Florence nursing home, my uncle once confided to me that he had reached his million-dollar savings goal. Other than paying the massive nursing home expenses, he never got to spend the money they saved. After his death, relatives on his side of the family fought over the estate. My dad was fond of saying he had never seen a trailer being pulled behind a hearse to carry money and possessions to the grave. Hubert Scott never figured that one out.

Bud Blanton would not have wanted any part of the life they lived. He would have spent his money and enjoyed his friends and lived a life punctuated with laughter. He would have encouraged his sister Edna to do the same. His advice would not have been heeded.

CLARISE

Clarise, my mother, was born in 1921. Her sisters could not agree on a lot as girls, but they expressed to me individually that Clarise had the sweetest temperament of them all. She was extremely smart in school, graduating in 1938 as valedictorian at Floyds High School. She could not afford to go to college. Instead, she married general store worker William Walker in 1940 and they had one son. She became the Nichols town clerk and assistant postmaster. My dad ran a corner grocery for many years and also worked in a U.S. Air Force commissary at Myrtle Beach Air Force base.

In their thirty-one years together, Will and Clarise were a happy couple who focused their love and attention on their only child; according to my aunts, they spoiled me terribly. Clarise valued education and got to see me become the first family member to earn a college degree. Sadly, she did not live to see the master's or the doctorate, both of which were dedicated to her. She loved decorating the Nichols Methodist Church with flowers and was one of the best-liked people in our town. She kept a picture of my uncle in the living room of our home and over the years I recall her breaking into tears many times at the mere mention of his death. She died of cancer in 1971.

After my mother's death, my father was inconsolable and became an alcoholic. Eventually he conquered his addiction. During the last years of his life, he was a motivational speaker and counselor for Alcoholics Anonymous. Late in his life he had a special friend, Ruth Ham, of Ketchuptown, South Carolina, and they enjoyed a happy friendship. On a bookcase, which I can see as I write this, is the familiar AA Code which he lived by the last decade of his life: "God, grant me the Serenity to accept the things I cannot change . . . Courage to change the things I can . . . and Wisdom to know the difference."

Will Walker died in 1988 after a years-long fight with cancer. To this day, I find notes he wrote to me in one place or another. He placed many of the notes he put aside for storage in the attic. The note in the bag with Bud Blanton's letters is one example. He left me a note and some coins in a safe deposit box I opened years after his death. I found a letter wishing me luck on my writing twenty years after he died. He left me keys and a note on which lock they fit. My guess is he knew that every time I found a note he would be with me for a few moments. I always enjoy looking through his old things, all of which I have saved. Each time I do, I hope to discover yet another note and share a moment with him once again.

Bud Blanton would have been at our house often because his sister Clarise adored him and his brother-in-law Will admired him. Bud loved to eat and Clarise loved to cook. He and Will would have been the best of friends.

BETTY

Betty Eloise Blanton was born in 1927. She married C. P. Mincey, a local farm boy, in November 1944. C. P. had volunteered for US Navy duty after graduation from Floyds High in the summer of 1944. Betty was an outstanding student. She remained in school after her marriage and was the valedictorian of the Class of 1945 at Floyds. C. P. came back from World War II, trained as a barber, and opened a shop in Nichols. From the beginning they were a happy couple. They had three children and Betty remained at home to raise them. Daughter Cindy was the valedictorian at Mullins High School in 1964 and later a teacher, school administrator, and finally local civic leader in Latta, South Carolina. The Mincey's youngest son Kenneth graduated from Mullins High, the University of Georgia, and the University of South Carolina Medical School. He is a surgeon. Their eldest son Charles was an all-around good student and athlete at Mullins High, graduated from NC State University in Engineering Operations and worked in the environmental field for major firms during his career. At family gatherings Charles assumes the role of master of ceremonies, prayer giver, and designated comedian. When asked about his career description for this book, he wrote with his typical humor, "You might want to add—Charles has turned down numerous chances to star in James Bond Movies but elected to continue to lead a quiet life out of the Public Eye!" He is named for my uncle and in some ways he is the most like him of anyone in the family. Bud Blanton's phrase for being silly was "to cut the fool."

Charles can do that on cue. Charles loves military history and Bud would have been his favorite uncle.

Betty Mincey has a photograph of Bud Blanton in the most prominent spot in her den and has spoken of him all the years I have known her. After my mother's death, she and C. P. remained close to my father during his troubled years as an alcoholic and became a second set of parents to me and Elizabeth.

In 2005, C. P. and Betty, along with their daughter Cindy and Betty's sister Sally, visited the tenant farmhouse near Duford in which the Blanton family had lived during the Great Depression and most of World War II. "The house was in bad shape," C. P. recalled. "They had been storing fertilizer and trash tobacco in the rooms and the roof was bad; it was just a mess." As the sisters reminisced about some of their happiest days at the house, daughter Cindy encouraged her parents to restore the house and not let it fall apart. C. P. agreed. It would be a present for Betty's 78th birthday, he decided. "I bought it from the owner that day," C. P. said. Shortly afterward, he had the six-room wood frame building with a gabled roof moved nearly fifteen miles to a farm the couple own in Marion County outside Nichols. "They had to cut the roof off to move it," he recalled. "But we got it set up on brick pilings and began to restore it." Within months they were sanding the original broad cut pine floors. And in less than a year they held an open house so family and friends could see the place they now call The Old House.

Daughter Cindy described her parents for a reporter: "They have always been about hard work. They had a mutual interest in doing this, and their excitement was evident. They are not faint-hearted, so no matter what obstacles they met, they were determined to finish."[1]

On holidays we gather at the Old House to celebrate as a family. Betty, C. P., their children and grandchildren and great grandchildren plus nieces and nephews and friends from all over come to share a meal and tell family stories. Their son Charles usually gives a prayer, and C. P. nearly always says a few words about the most beautiful girl he ever saw, his wife of almost eighty years. Then we sit down for a meal at the long table in the same kitchen where Bud Blanton spent his happiest days. This year, like all others, we will remember him and all the Bud Blantons in our land whose duty to country took from them the chance to live the life we enjoy today.

Figure 15. Betty Mincey's family in 2024. Left to right: Son, Kenneth; Daughter, Cindy; Son, Charles Fletcher; and C. P., the WWII sailor she married in 1944. Personal collection of the author.

Betty and C. P. have had the good fortune to live into their nineties, and it will be my great pleasure for them to read this manuscript which will become a book about our family. In other books I have written, I have told C. P.'s stories about growing up poor in Horry County, falling in love with Betty Blanton the first time he saw her when she was 13 years old, his time in the Navy on World War II convoy duty in the North Atlantic, and about life in general. He enjoys making fun of himself with his jokes. He and my aunt constantly work on projects around their house, farm, and local community. They are an inspiration to seniors.

C. P. knows my favorite story and tells it often. It is about the weekend when he was lovesick for my Aunt Betty and went absent without leave from the Navy at Norfolk, Virginia, and hitchhiked 250 miles home to Nichols to see her for two days. On the way back to Norfolk with my father, who was on approved leave, they had to change buses in Elizabethtown, North Carolina. They found only one seat available on the next bus. "Your dad Will was a petty officer and he knew I was AWOL," C. P. Mincey always tells his story. "So, he looked at that seat and said, 'C. P., you BETTER get on that bus.' I rode it back to Norfolk, crawled under a hole in the fence at the base and they didn't catch me. I know my brother-in-law Will saved me from a court martial."

My aunt and uncle are now both 97. He has asked that I speak at his funeral and in view of their longevity, I have asked that they speak at mine.

If Bud Blanton had survived the war, he would have spent a lot of time at the Mincey home. Betty was another sister who adored and admired him and, equally important, she knew her way around the kitchen from an early age. He would have spent hours with C. P. telling stories about Saturday nights in Tabor City and Fair Bluff and Mullins and riding around the countryside for fun with men and women friends. They would have laughed at C. P's stories of the Navy and tried to top each other describing the tough times each endured surviving the Great Depression. Eventually my Uncle Bud would have worn a military baseball cap like C. P. with "World War II Veteran" or "Timberwolf Division" emblazoned in gold letters above the bill. Like C. P., he would have been a member of American Legion Post 82 in Nichols. He, Willie Bishop, Jack Belcher, and that fourth man in their group whose name we have forgotten would have met regularly, to recall their time as Timberwolves.

SALLY

Bessie Evelyn Blanton was born in 1929. She got the nickname Sally as a girl and that was what we all called her. She married Lacy Lamar Gaddy of Timmonsville in 1948. Sally was the tallest of the sisters and a basketball player in high school. She finished Nichols High School in 1946 and went on to a successful career in business administration. Her husband Lacy, whose nickname in our family was Big Chick, was a soldier in World War II and returned to Timmonsville where he was in charge of the National Guard Armory. Big Chick Gaddy was larger than life, a stereotypical gravel-voiced old Army Sarge who convinced all of his nephews and nieces that he and Ike ran World War II from his duty station at Bury St. Edmunds, England. I fondly remember Sally Gaddy standing with hands on hips and a smile on her face in their home at Timmonsville. She was woman enough to see beyond Lacy Gaddy's rugged exterior and gruff manner and build a happy life with him.

Big Chick Gaddy's best stories came in late afternoon when he treated a mysterious, recurring leg ailment with shots of William Penn whiskey. To this day, when we speak of Big Chick's whiskey in the family, we call it leg medicine. And when he made his famous fish stew down on the Little Pee Dee River, William Penn was there also. According to my uncle, his bubbling stew was ready only when the William Penn bottle was empty. To all of us, he remains the one and only Big Chick.

The Gaddys had three sons. The oldest, L. L. Gaddy Jr., graduated from the University of South Carolina and the University of Georgia where he earned a Ph.D. in Biogeography. He can, and often does, talk a blue streak almost endlessly and, unlike many people, always knows what he is talking about. After university he established a career running his own environmental consulting firm and became a well-traveled and successful author. Although he grew to a burly 220 pounds plus, he has always been known in our family as Little Chick. Middle son Edward studied aerospace engineering at North Carolina State University and had a career in business to include ownership of a popular bike shop in Raleigh. Ed is also an accomplished pilot of powered and soaring aircraft. The Gaddy's youngest son Stanley has had a successful career in business and industrial plant management throughout the southeast.

Sally Gaddy for most of her life was a happy person, a loving aunt for her nieces and nephews. After a lifetime of telling fishing stories and war tales and consuming medicinal doses of William Penn whiskey, her husband Big Chick Gaddy died in 1984. Afterward, my aunt spent many happy years in Florence near her son Stanley and his wife Lynette. Sally Gaddy spoke to me often and fondly about her brother Bud. Her mischievous smile and good sense of humor brightened family gatherings for decades.

Unfortunately, the last two years of her life during the Covid lockdown and its aftermath were unhappy ones. For most of that period she was cut off from her family while residing in a senior living facility. She died in 2021.

Sally Gaddy, her sons, and Big Chick Gaddy would have been favorites of my uncle. He loved crowds and was at ease being with a group of people he knew. And when the conversation got going, and the William Penn started flowing for Big Chick, there wasn't a happier place around. My Aunt Sally would have hugged her brother Bud each time he came through her doorway because that's what big brothers are for and that is who she was, except for those last, awful months.

SON

My uncle Son was born Carol Huger Blanton in 1933. He was the good, dutiful son who was always up early to help his mother. As a boy he had weak spells which his sisters felt were the result of childhood asthma that was never diagnosed. After Bud went off to the Army, he stepped in to fill the void, assisting his mother in every way possible. As a boy his sisters called him Son. In later life his more popular nickname was Judge. This nickname came from his resemblance to his uncle, Judge Herbert Blanton. He graduated from Nichols High School and then married Eunice Turner in 1954.

Son went on to a successful career supervising custodial maintenance for a large firm in Columbia. Among my mother's siblings, he was the easiest to like from the first moment I met him. The asthma he suffered from as a boy contributed to his untimely death in 1980.

Son and Eunice had three children. Bob had a thirty-year career in the nuclear weapons complex at the Savannah River Nuclear Plant near Aiken, South Carolina. Hope had a career in hospital services. She died in 2007 of complications from an auto accident and lung disease. Karen continues a life-long passion for caregiving. My 90-year-old Aunt Eunice died in July 2024.

My Uncle Son would have revered his brother Bud had he come back from the war. He would have looked to him for advice and guidance. And in later years he would have been thrilled to proudly introduce his wife and their children to his big brother. They would have been the closest of brothers, loyal, loving, and kind to each other always.

RALPH

Born in 1936, Daniel Ralph Blanton was the baby of the family and even into adulthood was always considered that by his doting sisters. He graduated from Nichols High School and joined the US Air Force in 1955. He served overseas in France and Turkey as an Air Policeman. He came home and told us stories about being single in Paris, about Turkey and the Ottoman Empire, and life in far-away places. He was the person most responsible for instilling in me a desire to travel and see the world. In later years we were able to compare stories about working in both France and Turkey.

He married Joyce Norton in 1958. They had four children before divorcing in 1970. Infant daughter Joyce Ann was stillborn in 1959. Their eldest living daughter, Melinda Ann, became a social worker with a successful career in Washington State. Pamela Joy, who we called Pam, was a caregiver and accomplished basket weaver. She valiantly battled bone cancer the last decade of her life before succumbing in 2019. Son Danny Jr. suffered with asthma as a boy and a spinal ailment as an adult, but has assisted Ralph's widow, Helen Oakley Blanton, at Society Hill, South Carolina, since my uncle's death at 84 in 2020. Ralph's former wife Joyce remarried in 1970 and died in 2019.

I believe Bud would have been a tremendous influence on Ralph. Had he come home safely, he would have stepped in to be a father figure to both his brothers, particularly to Ralph, who was only 9 years old in 1945.

I am certain my uncle would have kept his promise to his mother to support her and the boys. All the Blanton children valued the bond common to family members who survived the poverty of the Great Depression. The boys would have supported one another without question. The example of the loving relationship of the sisters in later life and the support of their two remaining brothers makes that assumption a certainty. As older men, Bud, Ralph and Son would have grown increasingly closer. Ralph's more than twenty years of military service would have established a defining, additional, and unbreakable bond with his oldest brother.

DOT FLOYD

For the most important year of my uncle's life, Dorothy Mae Floyd of Nichols was the person he wrote most often, other than his mother. He wrote Dot as often as three times a day. And she responded, often writing him multiple times daily. For a year she was literally a family member. Dot was a Nichols girl, the oldest daughter of Jessie and Esther Floyd. She was born in 1928 and dated Bud before he went to the Army in the summer of 1944. She turned 16 on May 13, 1944, as Bud was preparing to enter basic training. Their dates often amounted to a drive to the movie theater on main street in Mullins and meetings with friends doing the same thing.

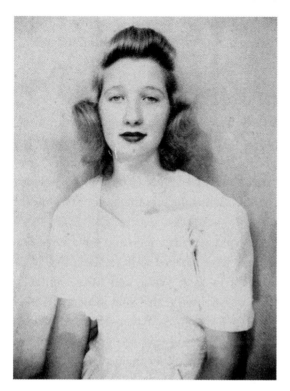

*Figure 16. Dorothy "Dot"
Floyd was the girl back
home who Bud Blanton
wrote daily. Collection of
the author.*

Nearly every one of his letters to his mother mentions her. As Betty Mincey
recalled, "Bud dated some girls but Dot was special."

Nearly two years after my uncle's death, Dot Floyd married a veteran
and local farmer Orton Grainger on December 7, 1946. They had two
daughters, Cheri and Nancy. Cheri was a classmate at Mullins High, but I
never knew the connection of her mother to my uncle until reading his letters. Nancy Grainger married a Mullins High classmate, Jerry Bane. Cheri
married an Army officer and I visited with them in Hanau, Germany, in
the 1970s while working at *Stars and Stripes*. Dot died in 1994, aged 66.
Cheri died after a second marriage. There was no obituary. Her sister
Nancy passed away in 2017. Her widower Jerry Bane is the chief executive
officer of First Citizens Bank in Mullins.

If Bud had lived, would he and Dot Grainger have married? I don't
know. She had a good life with Orton Grainger and two beautiful daughters. But I believe she would also have experienced a happy life with my
uncle. She was that special girl back home he talked about constantly to

his fellow soldiers. And even if they had not married upon his return, he would have always held her in special regard. She was, for him, the one.

But it was not to be.

WILLIE BISHOP

Willie Bishop, my uncle's wartime friend, lived a long, active, and interesting life. He became a member of the Blanton family by virtue of his friendship with Bud Blanton. From the day he first knocked on my grandmother's door in 1945, there was always a warm welcome in Nichols for him. Back home in Taylors, South Carolina, he was the father of a son and a daughter.

Willie married Helen Julia Fleming in 1937 and their son, Steve, became a golf pro in the 1950s. Steve later worked at NASA in Florida for thirty-five years. He died at age 73 in 2015. Willie and Julia eventually divorced and afterwards he had a daughter with Dolly Watson. Wendy Batey of Greer, South Carolina, is their daughter. "My mother and my dad had a loving relationship," Wendy said. "He always recognized me as his daughter. He was softspoken. He didn't talk about the war much. He was 50 and my mom was 30 when I was born in 1969. He gave me a ring he got off a German soldier's body and that's what I have of him. I never knew anything about the Blanton family."[2]

Kim Patterson was a married adult when her mother, Alice Bull, married Willie in the 1990s. "He was a gentle soul," Kim, of Easley, South Carolina, recalled. "Very kind. He stayed real close to the men of his troop in the Army. He attended their get togethers. He never said anything to me about the Blanton family and your uncle. But I know that he would be thrilled to death that somebody would write about what he did in the war. He was very proud of that and of all the men he served with."[3]

Willie Bishop had a successful career with Celanese Textiles in Greenville, South Carolina, and was an active sportsman and proficient golfer. He recorded thirteen holes in one during his years on the links. Among the photographs he left behind were several taken with fellow members of the Timberwolf Division at their yearly reunions.

Had my uncle lived, I am certain he would have been there at reunions with his true friend Willie and the other Timberwolves, young men from every corner of America who answered the call. Willie would have been one of the few people to whom Bud Blanton could have talked man to man about the war, about the friends lost, and how fighting their way across Europe changed them and the millions of service members who shared their common experience.

Willie left our family in 2007 at age 86, knowing he had kept the wartime promise made to his friend Bud Blanton. His first visit to Nichols and the lifelong friendship that ensued eased a mother's pain in a way no one else could. That, to me, is a magnificent way to be remembered.

THE LASTING IMPACT

The loss of a family member in war has a lasting impact upon families, friends, and, in many cases, entire communities. Military members who die while in service to their country, particularly in war, are honored with rituals, posthumous awards, and family stories passed from generation to generation. Like my family, the most revered photo on the wall in hundreds of thousands of American homes is that of a service member who gave the last final sacrifice for country. The same is true for the families of the fallen in most of the countries around the world.

Communities honor fallen veterans; they name American Legion and Veterans of Foreign Wars posts for them. Countless highways and buildings and parks honor them. And we construct grand monuments like the Vietnam Veterans Memorial wall to celebrate those who gave all. For me, the lasting impact is an emotional one that falls squarely on the individuals who remain behind, who must remember and grieve, often for a lifetime, as has been the case in my family. Sadly, the generational memory for Bud Blanton and the other soldiers who fell in World War II is fading. Like the World War II veterans who are leaving us at an alarming rate, those who remain behind and who treasure the memory of a fallen loved one are passing at the same fast pace. In researching the life of my uncle, I came to understand that I am close to the end of the line of those with personal memory of his siblings and his mother. I am among the last survivors who attended his funeral. Soon enough, other than the written word in this book, there will be little to remember Bud Blanton and most of the others mentioned from his war. The words chiseled on gravestones and markers will be all that remain for most. The men and women who did not come home alive from all our country's military experiences deserve better across this land. I hope and pray that someone after me will keep the flame alive for my uncle's sacrifice and the sacrifices of all the others like him. As a nation we have an obligation to remember and to honor those who enabled us to freely walk the path we have chosen.

CHAPTER 6

Bud Blanton's Friends Who Also Never Came Home

As every Europe front line infantryman knows, an egg would make the K or C rations pretty eatable. We also knew they were few and far between and you had plenty of competition for them. You had to move quickly and have a pretty good idea where to find them to get there first.

Towards the end of the war, we were moving quite rapidly. We came into this town and were going to spend the night there. I said to my runner, "Go and see if you can find any eggs. I hoped he might find a couple. I told him I would be held up here for about an hour until I got the platoon quartered and set up some type of defense.

In about 15 minutes he came back and said he found some eggs but couldn't get them. I said, "What do you mean you can't get them?" He said the hen house was locked and the owner was standing by the door and he couldn't get in. I said I would be done pretty soon and I would go with him.

When we got finished we went and found the hen house with 150 or more hens. There stood the lady guarding the door. I said in my best German, "Haben sie aire?" (Do you have any eggs?) She replied with "nicht versteha"(I don't understand). After two or three more attempts to make her understand, I raised my carbine getting ready to shoot the lock. She threw up her hands and loudly shouted, "Versteha, versteha (I understand). She whipped out the key, opened the door and gave the bounty to us.

The whole mortar section had 4 or 5 eggs each. I don't remember eating K rations that night.

I was telling this story one time and a lady asked if it bothered me to take the eggs. I said, "No, we were giving our lives. They were just giving eggs."

—*Paul Chronister, Company K, 413th Infantry Regiment*

A few minutes into a conversation with an elderly person from the Horry County crossroads settlement of Duford is all it takes to hear the first mention of the local young men who never came back from World War II. My Aunt Betty Mincey immediately recalled four or five servicemen including her brother Bud among the war dead. My research eventually turned up the names of eight other local servicemen who died in addition to my uncle. All but one of them were former students at Floyds High School, now Green Sea Floyds. Gary Blanton and my uncle's best friend Hayden Floyd were the first I heard about in interviews. And then the names of the others came in quick succession as I reviewed the casualty lists for Marion and Horry Counties.

DUD WATTS

In the 1950s I remember our neighbors Marshall and Orilla Watts often sitting on their front porch in Nichols staring blankly out at the corner of East Pee Dee and Averette Street. I now understand one reason for their somber mood. The couple sent three sons to World War II and only one came home alive.

Dud Watts was born May 31, 1919, and was living on Rural Route 2, Nichols when he registered for the draft October 16, 1940. He listed his uncle Pearson Gibson as his primary contact.[1] He entered US Army service June 13, 1942, and was killed August 5, 1944, in fighting at Papua, New Guinea. Watts, a private first class, was 25 years old and a member of the 503rd Parachute Infantry Regiment. His body was returned to the United

States in early 1949 and he was buried at Riverside Cemetery, across the Lumber River from Nichols, on February 7.[2]

BILLY WATTS

Billy Watts was born March 14, 1925, and registered for the draft March 16, 1943.[3] He listed his mother Orilla as his primary contact. He entered Army service December 20, 1943, and was wounded in action in France on September 1, 1944. He was killed in Germany on February 26, 1945. His unit was the 121st Infantry Regiment of the 8th Infantry Division. Billy Watts's death came a day after elements of his division finally took Düren on the far side of the Roer River not far from the place where Bud Blanton had been killed. He died three weeks before his 20th birthday.[4] His body was initially buried at Henri-Chapelle American Military Cemetery in Belgium before his remains were returned to his family in December 1947.[5]

I am certain Bud Blanton knew both Dud and Billy Watts. "Their family farm was not that far from us on Route 2, Nichols," Betty Mincey noted.[6]

A third Watts brother is also buried at Riverside Cemetery. First Sergeant Cole Watts spent nine years in the Army, enlisting first in Hawaii in 1937. His wartime service took him along the same route as Bud Blanton and his brother Billy Watts with stops in England, France, Belgium, Holland, and Germany. He died in 1961 and his widow Marie Strickland Watts passed in 2008.

Orilla Watts died in 1959 and Marshall Watts in 1985. The last of their children, Ethel, died in 2013.

VINCENT ASTOR FORD

Vincent Astor Ford graduated from Floyds High and joined the Marines in 1934 at the age of 20. He was the son of Boyd and Zonnie Moss Ford of Route 2, Nichols. He served with the Marines in Peking and Shanghai, China, before World War II and was commissioned a Second Lieutenant in 1943. His duty stations included the Philippines, the Caroline Islands, and Guam in the Mariana Islands. He was fatally wounded there July 21, 1944, and posthumously awarded the Silver Star for gallantry.[7] His citation reads: "For conspicuous gallantry and intrepidity as Mortar Platoon

Leader attached to the First Battalion, Twenty-Second Marines, First Provisional Marine Brigade, during action against enemy Japanese forces in the vicinity of Agat Village, Guam, Marianas Islands, on 21 July 1944. With the two assault platoons suffering heavy casualties under the fierce resistance of the Japanese, First Lieutenant Ford daringly moved forward to adjust his fire for greater effectiveness and, after making his way up the difficult route in the face of devastating hostile fire, was mortally wounded. . . . He gallantly gave his life for his country."[8]

Notification to the family came shortly afterward and October 27, 1944, *The State* newspaper announced Vincent Ford's death.[9] A photograph in the newspaper above the list of wounded, missing, and dead service members showed three Carolina Marines on Guam and a collection of Japanese swords taken during the fighting. The Marines were Sergeant Addis S. McGinn Jr., son of Mr. and Mrs. A. S. McGinn of Wilmington, NC; Corporal John W. Montgomery, son of Mr. and Mrs. J. H. Montgomery of Lancaster, South Carolina; and Private First Class Shuford L. Mabry, son of Mr. and Mrs. J. E. Mabry of Spartanburg, South Carolina.

The Silver Star was presented to Vincent Ford's parents in the family home May 18, 1945, in the presence of friends and relatives. At age 31 he was the oldest of the servicemen from the Nichols area killed in the war. He was buried first at Army, Navy and Marine Cemetery Number 2 on Guam. His family requested return of his body on August 26, 1947, shortly after the government extended the offer of repatriation. His reinterment service was October 26, 1948, at the Floyds Methodist Episcopal Church, with burial afterward at Riverside Cemetery. Pastor Charlie Hill presided over the services. The *Charleston News and Courier* obituary noted: "He was a member of the first group to land on Guam where he was killed shortly after the landing."[10]

FORREST FLOYD

Forrest Floyd, another soldier from Duford killed in action, was an upperclassman my uncle would have known in high school. His parents were Boyd and Emma Floyd of Duford. The *Florence Morning News* reported in his reinterment obituary December 17, 1947, that Forrest Floyd was killed in the Battle of the Bulge on December 25, 1944. "Private Floyd was one of his community's finest young men and possessed a sterling character," the newspaper reported. "He was born in Horry County December 8, 1923, and was graduated from Floyds high school in 1941.[11] At school he was outstanding in his work, having achieved the honor of valedictorian of his class. He was a member of Wannamaker Baptist church, entered Mars Hill College and studied there one year before entering the service on December 20, 1943. Services were conducted by Rev. J. L. Pierce, pastor at Forrest's church, Wannamaker Baptist."[12]

Forrest Floyd served with the 106th Infantry Division, which was activated at Fort Jackson, South Carolina, in March 1943, trained at Camp Atterbury in Indiana and shipped to England in late 1944 for more training. The division arrived in France the first week of December and entered Belgium on December 10. It was the fate of the division to be at the center of some of the bloodiest fighting at the start of the Battle of the Bulge. The 422nd and 423rd Regiments of the division were surrounded by the Germans at the start of the Bulge offensive, and 6,000 division soldiers surrendered December 19, 1944. The remaining division elements, including Forrest's unit, the 424th Infantry Regiment, were assigned December 20 to the XVIII Airborne Corps. The 424th then fought its way out of a German pincer movement and withdrew to the strategically important Belgian railhead town of St. Vith. Military historians say the heroic stand by the remainder of the 106th Division at St. Vith overturned the German timetable for taking the port of Antwerp and eventually disrupted the entire offensive. St. Vith and Bastogne became two of the most famous battles in the Bulge offensive.

After the successful delay of the Germans at St. Vith, Forrest's unit pulled back under heavy fire to an assembly area near Anthisnes, Belgium. It was near that town that Forrest was killed Christmas Day, 1944.[13]

Forrest Floyd's mother Emma wrote the Army Quartermaster General on January 9, 1945.

> I would like to get all the information available about my son, Private Forrest Floyd 34848511, who was killed in Belgium December 25, 1944. Did he regain consciousness after he was wounded? On what part of his body was he wounded and how long did he live after being wounded? I want all of his personal belongings

such as his Bible, watch, ring, letters and so forth if you can send them to me.[14]

There is no record within Forrest's personnel file of a reply by the quartermaster general or the unit Chaplain Alfred V. Bradley. Jessie Blanton received a letter from the chaplain who attended her son's body, but it was among the lost letters I found and not in Fletcher Blanton's official Army file. Chaplain Bradley retired as a lieutenant colonel in 1952.[15]

Forrest Floyd's remains were buried first at the Henri-Chapelle American Military Cemetery in Belgium, about eight miles from Aachen across the German border. His parents eventually received his personal effects, which included a Bible, souvenir coins, pictures, and some French and Belgian money. A check was issued to the family for $63.63 for the money found on his body.

The cemetery record from Belgium shows that Forrest's burial marker at Henri-Chapelle had been incorrect for the nearly two years his remains rested there. The disinterment directive noted, "Marker reads "Floyd Forrest" (Name backwards)."[16] Boyd and Emma Floyd asked that their son's remains be returned to the United States when possible and received a telegram November 21, 1947, announcing the shipment of his body. On December 12 the Floyds were notified by telegram that the body would arrive by rail in Mullins at 9:55 AM on Wednesday, December 17. Meares Funeral Home in Mullins made the pickup of the body on that day. The service was conducted the following day by Wannamaker Baptist Church Pastor J. L. Pierce. Burial followed at Riverside Cemetery.

Forrest's mother Emma Hooks Floyd died in 1966 and his father Boyd in 1972. Records indicate that all five of his siblings are no longer alive. The last to die was Eunice Floyd Britt in 2013. Forrest's brother Chester was a World War II US Navy veteran. He died in 1978.

LOTHAIR GODFREY

Another Floyds High graduate (1943), Private First Class Spurgeon Lothair Godfrey, served with the Third Battalion, 24th Marines of the 4th Marine Division in World War II. He was wounded in action but survived the war. He died November 25, 1945, at Honolulu. Lothair was the son of

Daniel and Grace Hayes Godfrey of Route 2, Nichols.[17] He was a student at Clemson College when he registered for the draft in 1943 at the age of 18.[18] His father told friends after the war that Lothair died in a swimming accident in Hawaii while trying to save the life of a friend and that both drowned. There is a gravestone for him at Riverside Cemetery complete with the words BURIED AT SEA and the inscription, *"Greater love hath no man than this, That a man give his life for his friend."*[19] His name is also inscribed on the memorial wall of the National Memorial Cemetery of the Pacific in Honolulu.

LEO HUGGINS

Private First Class Leo Huggins attended Spring Branch Elementary School and Floyds High School just like the Blanton children.[20] His parents, Maston and Vodie Powell Huggins, lived only a short distance from the Blanton farm. He entered the Army in 1942 and was killed in Normandy, France, on June 8, 1944, two days after the D-Day Landings. He was 19. His mother died less than a month before him, on May 13 at the age of 51, and was buried at Riverside Cemetery in Horry County.

For the next three years after Leo Huggins' death his family had to endure bureaucratic errors, which involved sending mail to his deceased mother. She and Leo's sister Evelyn had been listed as beneficiaries on his serviceman's life insurance policy. Evelyn, then 23, wrote to the Army on November 13, 1944, and reminded the Army that her mother was deceased. However, as late as July 1947 the Army was still writing Vodie Huggins at Route 2, Box 57, Nichols, South Carolina, to inform her of the status of repatriating her son's remains to the US.[21]

Leo Huggins was a member of the 175th Infantry Regiment, one of the three infantry regiments of the celebrated 29th Infantry Division, which came ashore on D-Day, June 6, at Omaha Beach. The 175th landed a day later with orders to take Isigny, a fishing village between Omaha Beach and Utah Beach.[22] Leo Huggins never advanced far beyond the outskirts of Isigny, and his remains were first interred at the temporary American military cemetery at nearby La Cambe.[23] Meanwhile, his unit participated in the battle for the town of St. Lo, the scene of some of the most bitter fighting in the Battle of Normandy.

*Figure 17. Bud's best friend
Ottis Hayden Floyd of Duford.
Collection of the author.*

Maston Huggins asked for his son's body to be brought home in 1948. His reinterment service was held at Meares Funeral Home in Mullins on May 22 with Reverend Charlie Hill of Nichols presiding. Burial followed at Riverside.[24]

OTTIS HAYDEN FLOYD

Initial research turned up little on my uncle's best friend, Ottis Hayden Floyd, son of Ed and Lutie Vencie Floyd, also of Duford. Online information indicated he had no surviving siblings. But the internet was no equal to my aunt Betty Mincey and her still formidable memory.

"Oh, yes, everyone called him Hayden and he really was Bud's best friend," Betty Mincey said. "The family lived there at Duford, just back from the crossroads, and his sister Betty is alive."

Fifteen minutes later I was on the phone with 91-year-old Betty Floyd Ray. I should have known the name because she was the longtime counselor at Mullins High School, which I attended in the 1960s. We talked and

*Figure 18. Betty Mincey and Betty Ray both lost brothers in
World War II. Betty's brother Bud was Betty Ray's brother
Hayden's best friend. Photo by the author.*

agreed to meet. And a week later, with Betty Mincey at my side, we drove
to the outskirts of Mullins where Betty Ray greeted us at the door of her
suburban red brick home.

I told her that Hayden was mentioned in Bud Blanton's letters home.
He had asked for Hayden's address in an earlier letter and December 28,
1944, had written his mother, "I got Hayden Floyd address now an I no
where he is fighting at. He is in the 3rd Army the 25 division and not far
from where I am." My uncle never learned that his boyhood friend had
been killed in France on November 22, 1944, the day before Thanksgiving.
Bud Blanton was in Normandy when Hayden died in eastern France.

Hayden Floyd was born September 6, 1923, and registered for the draft
June 30, 1942. He entered Army service November 29, 1943, at Fort Jackson, South Carolina and after training was assigned to the 104th Infantry

Regiment of the 26th Infantry Division. Elements of the 26th were fighting around Dieuze, west of Nancy, and took the town November 20. Hayden was killed two days later.

"I remember that time," Betty Ray said. "I think there were seven boys killed from the Duford and Nichols area. My brother died near a town I can't pronounce. He was listed first as missing in action. I was about 13 when the telegram came. A lady from the Nichols office bought the telegram. I want to think that was about the 17th of December. And about a week after Christmas we got another telegram that he had been killed."[25]

Hayden Floyd's remains were kept overseas for nearly three years. His military file shows that he was first interred in the temporary military cemetery at Limey, France.[26]

His mother wrote to the Army and asked: "can the cause of his death be determined in any specific way?" There is no evidence she ever got an answer, but his full military record listed his battlefield wound as a fractured skull.[27]

Eventually the family received Hayden's personal effects. The first item returned was a money order for $75 made out to his mother. Later a package arrived with a bloodstained prayer book, 20 photos, and other small items. Those additional items were a brown wallet, his social security card, a fountain pen, a French five-franc bill, and thirty-five US coins totaling $2.76.

His parents, Ed and Lutie Floyd, made a formal request July 22, 1947, that Hayden's body be returned for burial at Riverside Cemetery. It took over a year for the request to be fulfilled.

Hayden Floyd's coffin arrived at the Mullins Rail Depot on Tuesday, September 28, 1948, with a military escort. His journey was on the same Seaboard Air Line daily train from Charlotte that would bring my uncle home a few weeks later. Meares Funeral Home picked up the coffin and delivered it to the family home at Duford. At 4:30 that afternoon a memorial service was held at Wannamaker Baptist Church, followed by graveside services at Riverside Cemetery.[28]

"I really don't have anything from my brother," Betty Ray said. "Over the years and the moves and a fire we lost most of the photographs and papers. But I have my memories of him. He sent me a dollar once," she said.

"I know he only earned about $50 a month. It was a hard time when he died. I do have his Purple Heart and I have given it to my daughter Vencie for my grandson who graduated from Clemson as an engineer."

Like his best friend Bud Blanton, Hayden also left behind a girlfriend when he went to the Army: Ruby Floyd, the daughter of Bishop and Ethel Floyd of Nichols. She was the cousin of Dot Floyd, who wrote Bud Blanton regularly during his time in service. "It was years after the war before Ruby got married," Betty Ray said. "I kept up with her through Dot."[29]

"Very few people remember my brother now," Betty Ray said. "He was not one of these people that you would meet that was vivacious and outgoing. He was sincere and earnest. And when you got to know him, he was friendly. He wasn't the type to go over and speak to someone he didn't know."

She told me about her family's situation before the war: "Hayden probably dropped out of school to work on the farm.[30] That was the way it was in those days. Back then I thought I wanted to earn some money working on the farm, but my father used a simple trick to convince me I didn't want anything to do with the farm. My dad always grew five acres of cotton every year. And I wanted to make some money so I told him to let me pick cotton and he could pay me. He told me I didn't want to do that but I insisted. So he took me to the cotton field and left me there with a sack and went to the store. He came back after a good while and I had this little ball of cotton in the sack. I wanted to know how much it was worth and he said 'There's not enough to weigh.'"[31]

Betty Ray said there are two reminders of her brother that will remain after she is no longer alive. One is his namesake, grandson Hayden Maxey. And the second is the Purple Heart she gave daughter Vencie for her grandson. It is the Purple Heart awarded to Private First Class Ottis Hayden Floyd who gave his life for his country far from home and family on November 22, 1944.

GARY FRANK BLANTON

Gary Frank Blanton grew up on the family farm in Horry County not far from the Blanton Cemetery. He was Bud Blanton's classmate at Floyds High School and a cousin. He died in one of the fiercest and most controversial battles of World War II, the assault called the Battle of Rapido River, on January 20–22, 1944.

A May 10, 1945, story in *The State* confirmed Gary's death: ". . . Pfc Gary F. Blanton, serving with the infantry in Italy, who was reported missing in action since January 23, 1944, has finally and conclusively been proved dead. It is believed that Private Blanton was killed during the Rapido River campaign."[32]

The notice from the War Department came to his mother, Mrs. Dora Blanton Clemmons of Tabor City, North Carolina.

The article noted: "In addition to his mother, he is survived by five brothers, Cpl. Harry Blanton with the army in France, Private Wilbur Blanton with the army in Germany. A.O. Blanton of Greenville; James Blanton, of Nichols and Olin Blanton, Jr., of Tabor City, N.C.; three sisters, Mrs. Fay Brunsin of Sanford, Fla., Mrs. Troy Collins of Mullins and Mrs. Oscar Putman of Laurens."

"Private Blanton, 20, entered the army in 1942," the article continued. "He had been in foreign duty only two months when reported missing. He is the son of Mrs. Clemmons and the late Olin I. Blanton."

Gary Blanton's nephew, Franklin (Frankie) Carol Blanton, is today a prominent South Carolina businessman.[33] "Gary's body was never found," Frankie Blanton explained during an interview at the family home on the Horry County farm where Gary lived and worked before he joined the Army. "But his death was substantiated by Army forensics experts. There was not physical remains for a burial. He is on the Tablets of the Missing at the Sicily-Rome American Cemetery in Nettuno, Italy. I went there in 1998 and made a tracing of his name."

Frankie Blanton said a well-known photo from the Rapido River battle shows his uncle accompanying stretcher bearers. "Everyone in the family who has seen the photo is certain that is him," Frankie Blanton said.[34]

Gary Frank Blanton, born July 5, 1923, finished the 9th grade at Floyds High School in 1940 and then went to work full-time on his brother James Blanton's farm. Gary was a compact 5 feet, 8 inches, 154 pounds with blue eyes, brown hair, and a ruddy complexion. "He was already a man at 18," Frankie Blanton said. "I know this from hearing my father speak about him. He was solid and strong. A friend of our family, Roy Huggins, told

*Figure 19. Gary Frank
Blanton's portrait at
his nephew's home.
Photo by the author.*

me that Gary was strong as an ox and that everybody liked him. He loved
to ride horses and daddy did also. He had a girlfriend, Brittie Blanton, and
the three of them rode a lot."

Gary Blanton enlisted at Ft. Jackson, South Carolina, on November 19,
1942. In Europe he served with the 143rd Infantry Regiment of the 36th Infantry Division, then a part of the US Fifth Army commanded by General
Mark Clark. His unit was involved in the attempt to cross the Gari River
on January 20–21, 1944. The fighting along the river became known as the
Rapido River campaign. In a forty-eight-hour span the Regiment suffered
its heaviest casualties of the entire war. Gary's death came during that two-
day period. He was awarded the Bronze Star posthumously for his role in
the combat along with the Purple Heart.

"They lost about 1,700 men in two days and a lot of people to this day
don't think that the commander, General Mark Clark, handled the campaign very well," Frankie Blanton said. "When I went to visit the memorial

wall where Gary's name is inscribed at Sicily-Rome American Cemetery, one of the caretakers there told me that on the 50th anniversary reunion of the battle, everyone there would have liked to get their hands on Mark Clark."[35]

The Rapido River battle was a stinging, costly defeat for the US Army, and after the war there were complaints to Congress. Secretary of War Robert Patterson backed Clark's decisions, but a representative of the 36th Infantry Division, Colonel Miller Ainsworth, testified before Congress, opposing the eventual conclusions of the War Department and criticizing Clark.[36]

The Sicily-Rome Cemetery, maintained by the American Battle Monuments Commission, is a few miles inland from the landing site at Anzio where Allied Forces came ashore Jan. 22, 1944, in an amphibious assault aimed at the eventual capture of Rome, thirty miles to the north.

All five of Gary Blanton's brothers and three sisters have died, but one individual remains who knew Gary well. Brittie Blanton Strickland lives at her family home in Horry County. She was a classmate of Gary Blanton at Floyds High and they dated during their school years.

"Gary was a kind, nice person," Brittie Strickland recalled. "He wasn't a person that made conversation. But he was nice like most of the Blantons. He dropped out of school like many of the farm boys at that time. I went on and finished in the class of 1943."[37]

She said their dates amounted to driving to local towns with any friend who had a car. "That was before the war and no one had much money," she said. "But if we could get a car we would drive to Mullins or to Tabor City, North Carolina. There was a 10-cent movie in Fair Bluff, North Carolina and we would all drive over there to the movie theater.

"I'm 93 and I can forget some things," Brittie Strickland said. "But I kept up with Gary after he went off to war. I don't have any of his letters left, but there is something I do remember. My father and I were driving to Loris and we were going through Mt. Olive.[38] We stopped in at Mack O'Teul's store and he came out and said 'James Blanton just got a telegram. Gary is missing in action.' I broke down. Then the next day I went over to his house and his brother James came out and told me the news again."[39]

"I thought the world of Gary," Brittie Strickland said. "I doubt if a day has ever gone by in my life since then that I haven't thought about him. That's the honest truth."

Brittie Blanton eventually married another World War II serviceman, Hybert Neauzon Strickland, who served in the Pacific with the 3rd Marine Division and came back to Horry County after the war. They had been married sixty-four years at the time of Neauzon's death in 2008.

Frankie Blanton framed his uncle's medals and a tracing of Gary's name on the Tablet of the Missing at Nettuno. The display hangs on his living room wall. Frankie's father, James Blanton, built a nursery addition for the church at Mt. Olive and named it in honor of his brother. Clearly, his family and those remaining who knew him never forgot his life and sacrifice.

Thus, at the end of two months of research on the fallen servicemen from my own community, I finally had an understanding of the impact the deaths had on the small rural area from which all the young men came. Their homes had all been within a ten-mile area around the Duford cross-roads in rural Horry County. It was estimated by my aunt that only a few hundred people, at most, lived in the immediate area. So, in the span of a few months a significant number of young lives were removed from the future of the farming community.[40] These young men, who might have been leaders in their community, county, and state, were lost forever. Parents and family members were left to grieve and friends to wonder what might have been. And now individuals like me, all these years later, had but an inkling of their sacrifice. Without my uncle's letters I would never even have learned their names. Was it always this way, I wondered after the research? Are people like me oblivious to such losses? Are families left alone to manage the loss and move on? For the most part, that is the case. It had taken most of a lifetime and my own military service to come to terms with how blind we can be to such losses, some of them as close as a house down the street, as was the case with me.

From the moment I read the letters about my uncle's last days at Mariaweiler in the vicinity of Düren, I realized that there had always been a connection for me to Germany and even to the place that my uncle died. That connection had been because my father befriended a young German prisoner of war named Peter Batty during World War II. Peter had been captured by the Americans and ended up working at the end of the war in a US Navy Mess Hall at Norfolk alongside my father, a Navy Chief Petty Officer. Before I went further with Bud Blanton's story, I knew I needed to reach back fifty years across my own life, across my military service and time in Europe and tell Peter's story and his unique connection to my family.

CHAPTER 7

Peter Batty and the American Military Cemetery at Margraten

The terrifying sounds of combat! In battle and before, in-between, and after, the medics were always at the ready, anxious to tend the wounds and heal the hurts of the fighting men of the 104th.

Enlisted medical corpsmen—as conscientious a group as ever donned U.S. khaki to go forth into battle—trained as litter bearers, first-aid men, and technicians. Assigned to companies and aid stations in each regiment, they were ever ready to assist their fellow soldiers over the hump to the hospital or ease the way of the dying comrade to "the better land."

Physicians brought into the Army underwent rigorous training beyond their medical degrees. Medical Field Service Schools challenged them, tested their mettle, brought them face-to-face with the realities of combat.

Despite the hazards they were subjected to in areas where the wounded were being treated, the medics lived up to a tradition, formed in training in Oregon and Colorado, of thinking first of the wounded soldier, then of themselves. They took care of those who hurt, they saved the lives of many.

The medics were a team with the chaplains. The former offered physical and emotional assistance; the chaplains gave spiritual and emotional guidance. Both were supremely important to the

Timberwolf Division as it fought its way toward its record as the Division with the greatest number of continuous front-line days.

—*Frank L. Miller, Medical Detachment, 413th Infantry Regiment*

During the time the Timberwolf Division moved across the Netherlands and into Germany, my father, a US Navy Petty Officer assigned to Norfolk, Virginia, met and befriended Peter Batty, a 19-year-old German prisoner of war. Peter had been drafted into the German Army and was captured in the Battle of the Hürtgen Forest along the German-Belgian border in the autumn of 1944. He was shipped first to Texas and then on to Norfolk. He had experience as a butcher, as did my father, and they both ended up working in a mess hall on the Navy's Camp Shelton in Norfolk.

In one of the ironies of war, Peter was conscripted from his home area of Düren and lived through combat while Bud Blanton left his home near Nichols, South Carolina, and died near Düren on a snowy, winter day only months before World War II ended. I knew Peter Batty's name almost as early as I did that of my Uncle Bud. One of my first memories was of my father teaching me German phrases. *Wo ist der Bahnhof?* Where is the train station? *Was machst du?* What are you doing? *Ich heisse Wilhelm.* I am called William.

"I learned all this from Peter Batty," my dad would say when repeating the bits and pieces of German he still recalled. "He, Peter, was a good, young boy and I sort of took him under my wing," my dad recalled. "We had another guy, Sepp, an Austrian, working there also," my father once told me. "Sepp was a Nazi with a bad attitude. But Peter was still a boy. He was always smiling and optimistic and I know he was happy he survived the battle. You wouldn't know he was a prisoner. He worked alongside me just like everyone else."

When I was assigned to Germany as a soldier in 1969, my father asked me to find Peter Batty. I promised I would. My first try was when my mother came to visit in the summer of 1970. She and I planned a trip from central Germany across the Dutch border to the American Military Cemetery at Margraten, Holland. Although our trip included touring in Bavaria and a visit to Paris, it was Margraten she really wanted to see. It was the place her brother's remains had been buried from 1945 until 1948.

We left for Margraten before daybreak June 30, 1970, and arrived at the German border about 9:30 AM. Sitting in the line of cars I asked for mom's passport and she handed it over. I opened it and saw it belonged to my wife Elizabeth. My mother had picked up the wrong passport from the coffee table in the early morning darkness. The Germans, so strict on detail, would never let us pass, I was certain. But it was a three-and-a-half-hour drive home to Heidelberg, so I asked if she wanted to try and cross with the wrong passport.

"Yes," she said immediately. She had come 4,000 miles to see the first resting place of her fallen brother. And she wasn't going to stop because of the passport.

"Just look straight ahead and smile if the guard talks to us," I told her.

At the control point the German border official barely looked at the passports before waving us through. However, the Dutch border officer, with both passports in hand, leaned in the window of our small Opel Kadett station wagon. He looked hard at my mother and then at the passport picture of my wife Elizabeth, a 25-year-younger woman. He raised his eyebrows and in that moment I was certain we would be stopped.

"We're going to Margraten Cemetery to see where her brother was buried after World War II," I said before the officer could speak. "She has come four thousand miles to thank the Dutch for caring for him," I continued. I was pleading, still certain the officer would stop us. But after a few moments of looking at us, he nodded and handed the passports back. Then he saluted us, something I experienced only once more in a half century of crossing international borders.[1]

"We're not out of the woods yet," I told my mother. "We have to get back across both borders this afternoon. But if they stop us, we will have seen Margraten. So let's enjoy the day."

Margraten is a village of about 3,500 people in the Dutch province of Limburg, about ten miles from Aachen. It is world-famous because of the Netherlands American Military Cemetery on the outskirts of the village. This sixty-five-acre cemetery, like all those of the American Battle Monuments Commission, is an island of pristinely maintained American soil in a foreign country. About 8,000 American war dead are buried at Margraten.

The Dutch people have always had strong ties to the cemetery. Members of the local community began adopting the grave sites of dead US soldiers after World War II. And that tradition continues to this day through the Dutch Foundation of Adopting Graves.

I saved my mother's daybook from her visit and also the letter she wrote my father, who had refused to travel to Germany. She very much wanted my father to make the trip, but he told her he would not set foot on German soil out of respect for his brother Sheldon who had suffered shell shock fighting the Germans during the Allied landing at Salerno, Italy, in September 1943. Sheldon survived the combat but temporarily lost his memory and was returned to a Navy hospital at Norfolk. There my father visited daily and helped nurse him back to health.

In the bag with my uncle's letters I had found my mother's letter home about the trip. In it she wrote:

> Billy and I went to Margraten Cemetery as planned. I started to back out because I felt like I was living in the past. The cemetery was lovely beyond any words that I could say to express it. It was cold and we walked all around. There are 8,301 American soldiers buried here. I think everyone who can get to Europe should visit the National Cemetery to see how our government honors its war dead. I was choked up but as we got on back toward Aachen I decided that I must get myself back together. Billy didn't know that I was having to keep myself together.

On the return trip at the Dutch border, the customs officer waved us through without checking our passports. On the German side the officer looked at our little car and the two of us, glanced for a moment at the passports, and waved us through. Afterward, we breathed sighs of relief. Clarise Blanton Walker, a woman who had never even gotten a traffic ticket and probably never, ever committed an offense of any sort, spiritual or otherwise, had broken international law twice in one day, illegally crossing the German and Dutch borders without a valid passport.

Back in Germany outside Aachen, we stopped for a late lunch in the town of Weisweiler. I checked the bulky area phone book in a roadside booth looking for the name Peter Batty. There were Battys listed but no Peter. I promised my mother we would all come back someday and find

Figure 20. Margraten wreath laying, 2020. Photo courtesy of ABMC.

Peter if he were still alive. At that moment, without knowing it, we were less than three miles from his home not far from Düren.

But it would be another three years before I found him, and my mother would not live to meet him. She had been diagnosed with breast cancer and had a mastectomy in 1966, my junior year at Clemson University. The cancer returned in 1971, months after I left the Army and returned to South Carolina. She spent her final days at my Aunt Betty's home, where my aunt and uncle gave up their bedroom and helped care for her. I took time off from graduate school at the University of South Carolina and spent most of the spring of 1971 with her. Many times we talked about her trip to Europe, about Bavaria and King Ludwig's castles and Paris and old Heidelberg. But she made it clear nothing else for her compared to that day at Margraten, the place her fallen brother had first rested before he came home. She died May 6, 1971. She was 49. In her short but purposeful life she showed me, more than any other person I have ever known, what the enduring bond of family means. On a warm spring day with a background of dogwoods, her favorite, we buried Clarise Blanton Walker beside her brother and her mother.

CHAPTER 8

Finding Peter Batty

Our home backs up against farm land owned by an American generation of original German Homesteaders, the farm buildings arranged much in the old German tradition. The distance between our backyard and the adjacent Farmstead is a familiar one. It is about the same distance one small farm unit was from another in Germany, the distance we crossed so many times on a night attack or patrol.

In the winter, the air crisp and cold, the ground covered with snow, and the moon a little less than half lit, I find myself standing in our backyard looking across that distance. There seems to be movement around the buildings. Unexplained shadows come and go in the snow covered field. It is like being hypnotized. Then comes a smell I recognize in my memory . . . the smell of combat. No, not the smell of gun powder or of the usual farm-land odors, but something else. I have become convinced it is the smell of fear. I want to go back into my house, but I am for that moment transfixed.

After fifty years I am there. I will always be going back, as if there is something I left there. Like all of those from the Company, I left my youth there. My view of life and death, my understanding of what true comradeship is about, my values as to what is truly important, plus many other aspects of my life, will never be the same.

But most importantly, I left friends who were as close to me as brothers, buried on foreign soil.

The battlefield does not leave the infantry soldier just because he takes off his uniform. Its effect is engraved in us, and in some unexplainable and unforeseen way, changes our lives.

It is not as if we have spent the last fifty years dwelling on the war . . . WE HAVE NOT!!!

We came home, replaced our uniform for brighter colors, and set about working to restore our country to civilian life and pursuits.

We deliberately shut out the war, married and raised children.

Now we are retired and our minds start rewinding the memory tape. We gather together—the men of Company B and our wives— to discover it was just yesterday. We can now tell our wives, and our children and our grandchildren, the price of war, and the continued comradeship we have with those men who are beside us.

We are proud to have been infantry soldiers.

—*John Miller, Company B, 414th Infantry Regiment*

In January 1973 I joined the reporting staff of the European *Stars and Stripes* newspaper in Griesheim, Germany. My father finally overcame his objections to visiting Germany and agreed to come along with my Aunt Betty and Uncle C. P. that summer. My dad asked again about Peter Batty, and I promised I would do my best to find him.

At Norfolk with my father in 1944–45, Peter had talked about Aachen being the nearest city to his hometown. So I wrote the two largest Aachen newspapers, identifying myself as a journalist and the son of a World War II US Navy sailor seeking Peter Batty, the former prisoner of war at Norfolk, Virginia. The newspapers ran my letter and within a week the replies started. The first two letters were notes saying that the Peter Batty I was looking for was dead, killed in action. Within days another family wrote to say their Peter Batty had died on the Eastern Front. A fourth report noted that the family's loved one, Peter Batty, had been a prisoner of war in the Soviet Union and had never come home. He had been declared dead.

Sorry, the writer noted, there is no need to search further. Then, about three weeks after the first flurry of letters, I found a small envelope in my mailbox at *Stars and Stripes*. The top line of the return address jumped out at me. Peter Batty. I ripped open the envelope.

"I am Peter Batty," the note written in German began. "I have been in Norfolk and I remember your father William." Peter wrote that he lived in the village of Inden outside Aachen. He said he had a wife and two teenage daughters and worked as a foreman in a local factory. He gave a phone number, and I called him that afternoon.

"My father is coming to Germany and he wants to meet you," I told him in German.

"Yes, yes, I understand," he replied in English.

We made arrangements for the visit and two months later, shortly after Will, Betty, and C. P. arrived in August 1973, we drove three hours from central Germany to the Weisweiler exit on the Autobahn about ten miles outside Aachen. We covered the short distance into town in a couple of minutes and pulled up in front of the building with Peter's address. All along the street people were leaning out the open windows. A television crew waited at the door and a couple of additional reporters with recorders and notepads in hand stood by the camera crew.

A stocky, smiling man in his early 50s emerged with his wife and children and faced my father with open arms.

"William," he called out.

"Peter," my dad joyfully replied.

They embraced and most of the people looking on from their open windows broke into applause.

"Welcome to Inden," Peter said. He turned and said, "This is my family. My wife Anni and my daughters Monika and Evelyn."

His wife and daughters seemed astounded that Peter was speaking English. And his daughter Evelyn whispered in his ear. Peter translated for everyone. "She said she had to study English all these years and I never told her that I could speak English. I told her it is the first English I have spoken in almost twenty-seven years."

Peter had learned about Bud's death from my dad in 1945. "They said then it happened near Aachen," Peter told us later over coffee and cake in the family apartment. "In 1945 I don't think I told him that where your

Figure 21. Reunion with Peter Batty at Inden, 1974.
Personal collection of the author.

uncle died was near where I came from," Peter explained. "But I told William and Betty and C. P. today that it was only about ten kilometers (six miles) from where we were then."

The television reporter interviewed the two men. "We were young then, just doing a job together in the mess hall," my father told the interviewer.

"William was kind to me," Peter Batty said. "He helped me. You could see he was a good person."

The reporters finally left and for two hours the two men reminisced about their years since Norfolk.

Peter's youngest daughter Evelyn again expressed surprise as her father carried on conversations in English with my father, Betty, C. P., and my wife Elizabeth while speaking German with me.

"Papa, you should have told me you speak English," Evelyn chided him again.

Peter reverted to German, speaking to me. "Tell them I think it was good to be alive then in Virginia, but what happened afterward as a prisoner of war in England brought back bad memories," Peter said. "Speaking English reminded me of that so I did not do it for a long time."

When he left Norfolk, Peter Batty thought he was being returned to his homeland. Instead, he was sent to England. "I worked for another year as a prisoner on an English farm," he said. "They had no food and they did not treat us well. I don't have a good memory of that time. It was not like being with William in the mess hall."

"I have something," Peter said. "Wait and I will get it." He came back moments later with the 1944 Thanksgiving menu from the US Navy Armed Guard School Shelton at Norfolk. "So much food," Peter said. When I found the bag of letters in the pie safe, one of the items saved by my dad was the 1943 Christmas Dinner Menu from the same mess hall. At the top my father had written to my mother, "P.S. Save this Hun, Love Will."

I wrote my own story of the visit with Peter. It appeared in *Stars and Stripes* and also *The State* newspaper.[1]

Peter visited the US with his wife and family two years later. He met both the Blanton and the Walker sides of the family. He paid his respects at Bud's grave and became a close friend of nearly everyone he met. Peter had been only a year younger than my uncle, and I felt that when he was visiting us in the US my family understood he had been lucky enough to survive while Bud had not. There was never any resentment about him once being a German soldier. And my family liked Germans and Germany because they liked Peter and Anni and Monika and Evelyn. Knowing Peter simply deepened my love for postwar Germany and the resilient, hard-working people like him who rebuilt their land from rubble.

Elizabeth and I stayed in contact with Peter, visiting him and his family many times over the next three decades. My reporting work occasionally took me along the *Autobahn* near his house while en route to cover stories in the Netherlands and Belgium. And I always made a fuel stop at the Esso station on the outskirts of Inden. The station owner knew Peter and he began to greet me with a smile and the comment "*Passt auf. Der Ami ist wieder da*"—Attention, the American is here again." When the Batty's oldest daughter Monika married a couple of years after our first visit, I sat with the family at the wedding and at the head table afterward. Peter's wife Anni died of brain cancer on their 38th wedding anniversary May 16, 1978. We met often in Europe over the next decade and in 1988 he flew to the US to make a last visit with my father who was by then bedridden with his advanced cancer.

During Anni's illness, Peter was befriended by one of the hospital nurses, and a few years later he became a companion to Nurse Elisabeth Bohlmann, who he called Lisl. Eventually Peter and Lisl visited our family in the US also.

"My father almost never spoke about the war," said Monika Batty Hörschkes, one of Peter's two daughters. "But when he got the letter and saw your father again, he was delighted and happy."[2]

"He did tell us after the visit of your family that he had been a war prisoner and that he met William and that he was also in England as a prisoner, nothing more," said his other daughter, Evelyn Batty Glasmacher.[3]

Elizabeth and I returned to the US in 2012 after forty years in Europe, and a visit with Peter and Lisl was the last stop with old friends before our return.

Peter's last comment to me was about his experience as a prisoner of war. "The time in England was not a good year," he told me. "They were not nice to me like William and the Americans. I like Americans." His health began to deteriorate not long afterward, and Lisl called me February 5, 2014, to say he had died as she nursed him. He was a month short of his 89th birthday. His death announcement in the local newspaper at Alsdorf-Busch near Aachen began with a familiar German saying. Translated, it read "When the sun sets on life the stars illuminate the memory." My parents would agree.

Like most service members who have been in combat, Peter didn't talk about the war voluntarily. I know he had no choice in entering military service. He told me it was duty to country, not to any political leader or ideology, that forced him into uniform. He was a young man when captured and, although he never said it, I believe he was relieved to be out of the fighting.

My understanding of what American service members faced in World War II is shaped to a large extent by what I learned from the men who served on both sides of my family. Foremost were the examples of my father and his brothers, Harry Lee, Joe, Sheldon, and Jimmy. I consider them all heroes although their wartime paths were decidedly different. On the Blanton side, I looked up to my Uncle Bud, who I never met, and my Aunt

Betty's husband, C. P., who has played a large role in my life from an early age. As a young man, I saw, too, the example of C. P.'s brother, Euel Shelley, who was drafted into service out of Clemson and served on the front line in Korea.[4]

Harry Lee Walker was a merchant marine sailor who served on convoys to Russia, and in particular to Murmansk. It was some of the most dangerous duty in World War II as the convoys suffered terrible losses on that particularly hazardous route.[5] Uncle Harry was one of the most agreeable individuals to be around and a wonderful storyteller. But I believe the stress of his wartime experience ground on him in later life. There was the influence of alcohol also. This was a time when posttraumatic stress disorder (PTSD) was not much discussed, but I think it played a role in how he lived his life after World War II. He was a trained plumber and did that work for many years. During his last years he worked intermittently when his health permitted. He died of cancer in 1960 at the age of 50.

Joseph Pyrum Walker was a US Navy radio operator and signals specialist in World War II. He served in a bomber squadron, which operated in the Dutch East Indies, New Guinea, and the Philippines. He was highly decorated, holding a half dozen Navy combat citations including the Air Medal with multiple clusters plus the Navy Air Crew Ribbon with two stars and participation ribbons in the American and Pacific Theaters during the conflict. After the war he was an electronics and electrical specialist. He rarely discussed his wartime service with any of his nieces and nephews, although he confided in his brothers who had similar experiences. His life was shortened because of alcohol. I believe that PTSD weighed heavily on him and thwarted his attempts to get his life in order during the later stages. He was born in 1923 and died of cancer in 1977. He was 54.

Sheldon Avery Walker was a US Navy combat veteran who saw action in the invasion of North Africa and Sicily and the landing at Salerno, Italy, where he was injured and reported missing. He also served with the British 8th Army in North Africa.

When Sheldon first came back to the Navy Hospital in Norfolk from his frontline duty, he did not recognize my father. He suffered from combat trauma, the Navy doctors told my father, who then visited Sheldon every day until his memory eventually returned.

Figure 22. Joseph P. Walker,
decorated Navy radio operator,
during World War II. Personal
collection of the author.

After the war my uncle was ordered along with many fellow sailors to watch the nuclear weapons tests at Bikini Atoll in the Pacific. These men were human guinea pigs, and the tragic result of their exposure to radiation was not revealed until many years later.

Sheldon Walker's daughter, Cheryl McClellan, said, "Daddy spoke of the radiation testing as being a wild experiment. The sailors were sent on deck in just their skivvies to observe the explosions. Afterwards, a group of scientists came aboard in hazmat suits with Geiger counters in hand. They scanned the sailors to read the amount of radiation to their bodies."[6]

Decades after the tests, the US government began making payments to the nuclear test survivors who had developed many types of cancer over the years. Many test veterans with cancer did not survive long enough to receive a payment, although eventually their families were authorized compensation.

Sheldon was a jolly person, the funniest and most social of the Walker brothers. He loved his family and was proud of his wartime service. I

Figure 23. Sheldon Walker in Naval uniform. Personal collection of the author.

know he was injured in combat at Salerno,[7] but he never spoke of it to me, and only in private moments with my father did he go back to those dark times. I also don't know how he felt about being ordered to watch the tests at Bikini Atoll in the Pacific Marshall Islands, but my family is certain he developed cancer because of that exposure.

Sheldon was a man of highs and lows, and his service in World War II weighed heavily on him. I loved to be in his presence during the highs. His daughter Cheryl said, "There were many nights in my teens that dad, having drunk more beer than he could handle, felt it necessary to wake me up and share of his sadness and madness of what the Germans had done. I know he contracted malaria in North Africa in a separate incident. When shipped home to recover, he weighed less than 100 lbs."[8]

My cousin Larry Walker, also a writer, was closest to Sheldon among the nieces and nephews.[9] I asked what he knew of our uncle's wartime trauma. He said, "Uncle Sheldon visited me at our apartment some 50 years ago . . . so I could interview him about his experiences in the war. We drank beer and talked for several hours. He was a sailor in the 'First Beach

Battalion', and those guys worked closely with, and may have been part of, the 'Seabees'. They came in to shore early, helping to clear beaches of obstacles, mines, etc., to help pave the way for an invasion by army troops. It was of course, perilous work, and casualties were high. . . . Uncle Sheldon described being on the beach at Salerno not long after Army troops began coming ashore. He said one of his fellow sailors had captured 2 or 3 Italian prisoners, and brought them up to where Uncle Sheldon was talking with an Army Sergeant. The sergeant was armed with a 'Tommy' gun, a Thompson .45 sub-machine gun. When the sergeant saw the sailor come up with the prisoners, he told him to move away from them, and in Uncle Sheldon's words, 'He cut them right in two with the tommy gun!' He began sobbing when he told me about the sergeant killing those Italians.

"He told me about riding on the back of an ammo truck, not inside the back of the truck or the cab, but standing on the back bumper and holding on, headed somewhere up the beach, when a German shell hit the truck. Uncle Sheldon said it blew him off the back, had he been riding inside it would have killed him. He was knocked unconscious for some time, how long he didn't know. He said he knew he had gotten a severe concussion, and no telling how that affected him and his behavior since the war. Sometime after that, he said he contracted malaria, at which time he almost died. Mama told me that after he got back to Wilmington, the two of them were in a movie together one afternoon, when news film footage came on about the war, Uncle Sheldon literally ran out of the theater"[10]

My father at first refused to travel to Germany to visit me because of his brother's experience fighting the Germans and Italians at Salerno. But he relented and later Sheldon also came overseas to visit along with my Aunt Joan. It was the happiest I had seen him in all the years I knew him.

Larry Walker also recalled, "When Uncle Sheldon was diagnosed with terminal cancer, I think it must have been early in 1981, 6 or 7 months before he passed, he got a new enlisted man's Navy Blues uniform. . . . One thing he didn't get were the ribbons he earned in World War II. At any rate, it was my honor to get these awards for him, that he had honorably earned thru blood, sweat and tears, in mankind's greatest conflict. I recall being at their house off Milton Road one winter evening. He asked me to join him, and he put on that uniform with the ribbons, proud as a peacock, and asked Aunt Joan to take some pictures of him with her camera. Keep in mind Uncle Sheldon was also a soldier in the US Army at Fort Jackson in the 50's, but his heart and soul of military service, and where his pride harkened back to, was as a youngster in Navy dungarees on those beaches in North Africa, Sicily and Salerno, where he carried a rifle and .45, and was almost killed. Though that war had traumatized him as it did millions of other Americans, he instinctively knew he had been a part of something far greater than himself, and that he had done his duty in keeping western civilization free."[11]

Sheldon Walker died July 4, 1981, at the age of 57. He is buried at Riverside Cemetery in Horry County. His daughter Cheryl recently added a postscript to her father's life: "My cousin Jay Walker encouraged Mama to reach out to the law firm serving veterans of radiation exposure. Dad's claim was accepted and sadly after all the red tape, the settlement was awarded in Sept. 2013, but only after mama's passing in July 2013." Cheryl and her husband Gary eventually bought a home near the North Carolina coast using the settlement money. They named their river home 'Joan's Bikini'.[12]

James Laurence Walker was the hero of my youth. He enlisted first in the Army in 1940 and served a year as a clerk at Fort Jackson, South Carolina, before being discharged in late summer 1941. After the attack on Pearl Harbor, he enlisted again and became an Army Air Corps pilot who served in the China-Burma-India theater. Jimmy Walker flew the Hump, the route across the Himalayas between India and China, during the war. He lit up my father's life each time he visited our home in Nichols after the war. I recall him talking now and then about the wartime flying because my father was also a pilot. But there was never boasting, just a retelling of events, sometimes humorous, sometimes sad. He was a successful cleaning products salesman after the war and continued flying as a major in the US Air Force reserve. I don't think the war weighed as heavily on him as it did Harry Lee, Joe, and Sheldon, but it was certainly there behind that quick smile. To fly the treacherous Hump Route for over a year from September 1943 to October 1944 meant that he faced his own mortality each time he took a military cargo plane to 20,000 feet through the treacherous passes between northern India, across Burma, and into China and back again.

His son Larry recalled: "One story Daddy would tell me when he'd been drinking, and I heard it several times, was the time he returned from

Figure 24. Jimmy Walker's portrait. Personal collection of the author.

a flight to Kunming, in Yunan Province, China, back to his base at Chabua, Assam Province, India. He'd get real emotional about it, and begin crying before he could finish the story. He was coming in for a landing, but learned an aircraft had just crashed ahead of him while landing, and was burning furiously on the runway. As his C-46 was getting low on fuel, he had to make the landing, or risk crashing himself. He had no choice. He said, through tears, 'We came in right through the flames, and made the landing, knowing those other guys were all dead!'"[13]

From my few talks with Jimmy Walker, I feel the military provided him with the happiest time of his life. But that came after his service overseas in his role training new C-46 pilots in Nevada. He was newly married to Mary Elizabeth Hewlett Walker, my Aunt Lib, and that time in Reno was one of the high points of their life together. Later, he enjoyed watching their three children, my cousins Larry, Jay, and Sharon, grow into successful adults. But I always sensed a wistfulness about him, about the good times past, particularly the time instructing after the real war. His oldest

Figure 25. Jimmy Walker (left) before a Hump flight. Personal collection of the author.

son Larry recalled, "His smile and wit were infectious. His nonchalant attitude when diagnosed with terminal colon cancer in 1971, was typical of his play the cards you're dealt attitude toward life."[14] Jimmy Walker died of cancer in 1971 at age 51. My Aunt Lib died in 2018 at the age of 94. They are buried together at Wilmington (North Carolina) National Cemetery.

My father, William Walker, was affected by wartime service more than his brothers ever knew. He felt a sense of guilt that he was never sent overseas while his brothers served in war zones. He trained as a gunner and his ship made practice runs in the Atlantic but he was never deployed. He was a good sailor and was named the top enlisted man in his unit at Norfolk. He was a role model to many in his unit. And I am certain he was a mentor to POW Peter Batty who was assigned to work with him.

After the war he ran a corner grocery, was a factory worker and finally worked as a meat cutter for the US Air Force in a life punctuated by hard work for relatively low pay. He loved to fly airplanes and was an accomplished Civil Air Patrol search pilot. He had a low period for years after my mother's death in 1971 and drank heavily. However, he recovered and spent the last ten years of his life trying to help others understand alcohol abuse.

Will Walker died of cancer, like all his brothers, in 1988 at the age of 73.

From my early years onward, I knew first hand that the Walker brothers all had their demons from the war and, to an extent, all used alcohol as an analgesic to dull those memories. It is hard to imagine that my Uncle Bud would not have brought home his own demons and been forced to deal with them. However, as noted earlier, in the letter to his mother, dated November 26, 1944, he wrote, ". . . I am not ever going to start back drinking." I believe he would have been able to keep his promise.

That leaves me and the impact of my military service. Despite my nearly two years in uniform, I have felt for half a century a lingering sense of guilt for having been sent to Germany instead of Vietnam. Like my uncle as an Army private, I had no control over my fate from the day I was drafted on March 3, 1969. But in November of that year, while serving at Fort Bragg, doing lawn mowing and kitchen police duty between days spent as a military writer, I received orders for Germany. That month, according to the military grapevine at Fort Bragg, nearly 500 soldiers were assigned to Vietnam and two went to Germany.

Military duty in Germany changed my life for the better, gave me an international outlook, and enabled me to pursue a writing career in Europe. I spent nearly thirty years with the newspaper *Stars and Stripes* telling the stories of Armed Forces members all over the world. They are, for me, the best people on Earth and I always feel privileged to be among them. But to this day, I feel I don't measure up to other family members like my cousin Ben Brown who volunteered, became a Green Beret, and spent much of his overseas year in Vietnam and Cambodia on dangerous long-range patrols. He came home, finished college, married Sue Page, had two outstanding children, Page and Benjamin, and was a successful building materials plant manager. He died in 2011 at the age of 65. Cancer again. And my cousin Larry, son of Jimmy Walker, joined the Marines and spent a year in Vietnam. He is the Walker family rock and has the most steadfast devotion to the value of military service of anyone I know. And Larry's brother, my cousin Jay, served in Iraq and was wounded there.

After my Uncle Bud, the individual I respect most for his military service is not a relative, but a lifetime friend. Barney Easterling and I went to Clemson together. We came from small South Carolina towns and had similar experiences in our youth. I liked him instantly. Barney ended up in the Army also and was sent to Vietnam. There, as a medic in the field, he saw things that would trouble anyone. He put all that aside when he came home, married Louise Marshall of Kingstree, and began a highly successful business career there. He retired a few years ago and has confided that he still remembers things from that year in Vietnam, things that would disturb any feeling human being. I respect him for sharing that. I have never told him until now that he is also one of my heroes. And like most of the men in D Company and all the Walker brothers and C. P., Euel, Ben, Larry, and Jay, hardly anyone will ever know how they answered the call. But I know. And that counts for something.

CHAPTER 9

The Timberwolves

One afternoon as we were on the big push toward the Mulde River to meet the Russians, it was getting near twilight when we spotted a small village ahead. The Chaplain (Capt. Clair F. Yohe) said to me, "Let's hurry up and try to find a place with a window if possible, before they all are taken by the troops so we won't have to sleep outside tonight in the cold."

We progressed along the road for a short distance when I saw some of the boys from the line companies that I recognized lying in a ditch along the road. Soon a lieutenant stepped out on the road and stopped us and asked us, "Where are you going Chaplain?" We replied, "Why, we're going up to that town to try to get a place to sleep inside tonight, if possible." The lieutenant responded, "It would be best if you wait a while. You see, we are going in to capture that town as soon as it gets dark."

—O. B. Spencer, Service Company, 414th Infantry Regiment

April/May 1945. The war was nearly ended. Our outfit was on the move, seldom staying in any spot for more than a few days, so I have no idea where we were. I'm sure that most of us privates had the same feeling—obey orders and live one day at a time.

The roads were crowded with hundreds of peasants, U.S. soldiers and airmen and German prisoners of war. They needed to be moved from the open fields where we found them to facilities where they could be sheltered and fed. I made many trips on these assignments

to move people, after removing ammunition, supplies and most
personal gear from the back of my truck. The displaced persons
from Poland, Russia, Czechoslovakia and various other southern
European countries had been enforced workers for the Germans. I
did not see any that looked like they had been starved or beaten, but
they were thin and poorly dressed.

Then there were our U.S. soldiers and airmen who had been
prisoners of the Germans. They came by the hundreds. In a number of cases I was the first American they had seen in months. They
had been marching to the east and then to the west as the Germans
tried to keep them away from active front lines. Food had been at a
minimum and they had frequently made do with turnips or potatoes
from the nearby fields. They were dirty, skinny, and appreciative. I
usually had a couple of bottles of looted wine in my pack. The first
bunch of freed prisoners took care of that. Also they eagerly con-
sumed any rations that I had brought along that day.

—*Richard S. Graff, Headquarters Company, 2nd Battalion,
415th Infantry Regiment*

Private First Class Fletcher Blanton's Timberwolf Division was vital to the
Allied conquest of the Nazis and the final drive into the German heartland.
The 104th Infantry Division, which my uncle joined as a replacement in
late 1944, was activated September 15, 1942, at Camp Adair, Oregon. The
division insignia of a grey wolf head on a green background was adopted
with the name Timberwolf Division. The unit trained in Oregon, California, and Arizona before being shipped to the European theater.

Major General Terry de la Mesa Allen took command of the division
on October 15, 1943. Allen was a no-nonsense, decorated World War I veteran and had commanded the 1st Infantry Division in North Africa and
the Mediterranean area in World War II before returning stateside to lead
the 104th. The Timberwolves embarked for France on August 27, 1944, and
arrived in Cherbourg on September 7. Two of the division units, the 415th

Infantry Regiment and the 387th Field Artillery Battalion, landed at the artificial port set up alongside Utah Beach, down the Cotentin Peninsula coast from Cherbourg.

The division marched to the railhead at Valognes and then was shipped by train to the Antwerp area where it moved into the front line alongside Canadian troops. For the next six months, elements of the division would be involved in combat every day as they breached the Siegfried Line and moved through Germany.

Only hours after Bud Blanton's death at Mariaweiler on the Roer River, the division suffered a friendly fire attack. The accidental bombing killed at least 28 Timberwolf soldiers. Corporal Dallas R. Queck, a member of the division's 104th Reconnaissance Troop, recalled the death of his friend Malte Lundell and the other soldiers during the attack. "It was Jan. 10, 1945 and we were bivouacked in factory buildings in the industrial city of Weisweiler," he reported,

> We were waiting to make the Roer River crossing. The Germans had destroyed a Dam upstream. That plus heavy rains had swollen the river, and the air corps thought it was the Rhine River and bombed the area with bombs they still had in their bomb bay. Malte was manning a 50-caliber machine gun on the top of a slag pile and was fatally injured. In all there were 28 men killed and many wounded, but Malte was the only one in the Recon who was a casualty. For myself, I normally played cards with a group but the place we would have played was not available because that soldier had gone AWOL, and so we went back to our separate areas. That gathering place was flattened by the bombs. How lucky can you be!!!!![1]

Private First Class Daniel Ponzevic, a Timberwolf Division member from the 320th Engineer Battalion, also lost a friend, Al Gates, in the friendly fire bombing. Gates had been Ponzevic's tentmate until he was transferred to division headquarters to run a generator. Ponzevic recalled the day Gates and the others were killed:

> Soon word came, "Mount up, Division Headquarters has just been bombed by 17 to 20 bombers. They need our help." Someone at

headquarters had been listening to their radio chatter when he heard "Bombs Away." Soon after, the sticks of bombs were exploding all over. The planes might have aborted from their initial target and decided to dump their bombs on a target of opportunity. But why us? Headquarters was located in the power plant area for over a month. The plant had four huge tall distinctive smokestacks. Further, there were two rivers between it and the ruins of Düren, which these bombers may have visited. Weather was clear and visibility was excellent. Friendly fire? How sad to be killed by your own.[2]

The division defended its position along the Roer River until late February 1945 when it began the advance that reached the bombed-out Rhine River city of Cologne on March 5. The division participated in the encirclement of the German Ruhr region and took Paderborn on April 1, 1945, then advanced east and crossed the Weser River on April 8. The official 104th history notes:

The Division then crossed the Saale river and took Halle . . . in a bitter five-day struggle 15 to 19 April. The sector to the Mulde River was cleared by the 21st, and after vigorous patrolling, the Division contacted the Red Army at Pretzsch 26 April. Contact with the enemy was lost on 5 May, completing 195 days of combat.[3]

The Timberwolf book, *War Stories of WWII*, gives a more detailed account of the end of the war:

On 30 April, 1945 Russian troops southwest of Berlin, Germany fired on a small patrol from the United States 104th Infantry Division. When the patrol released green flares, the prearranged signal, and raised the American flag, the Russians realized their mistake, lay down their arms, and joyously joined their allies in celebration. That same day, less than 25 miles away in Berlin, Nazi leader Adolf Hitler and his new bride killed themselves hours before the Russians planted a flag atop the roof of their underground bunker. In one week the Third Reich would surrender unconditionally and World War II would be over in Europe.[4]

The Timberwolf Division left Europe at the end of June 1945 and was inactivated December 20. During World War II seven units of the 104th were honored with Distinguished Unit (Presidential) Citations.

Two Timberwolves were awarded the Medal of Honor. First Lieutenant Cecil H. Bolton was decorated for conspicuous gallantry during a night battle November 2, 1944, following the crossing of the Mark River in Holland. Private First Class Willy F. James Jr. posthumously received first the Distinguished Service Cross and then in 1997 was awarded the Medal of Honor by President Bill Clinton.

The 104th lists the following statistical account of its actions in World War II:

> During the 195 consecutive days of combat the Timberwolves had inflicted upon the enemy over 18,000 casualties in killed and wounded; captured over 2,000 towns and communities including the great cities of Cologne, Eschweiler and Halle; had taken 51,724 German prisoners, including four generals; 1,301 officers; 5,397 non-commissioned officers, and 45,022 other soldiers. In clearing over 8,000 square miles of Belgium, Holland and Germany, the 104th Division had left behind 1,447 comrades, whose supreme sacrifices on the battlefield had contributed so materially to our success. In addition, 4,776 had been wounded and 76 were reported missing in action.[5]

After the war the National Timberwolf Association was formed. Annual reunions brought together thousands of the more than 34,000 men who served in the division during the war. The final Timberwolf reunion was held in 2010, and the formal organization of the association ended March 1, 2013. The National Timberwolf Pups Association was formed by the sons, daughters, families, and friends of division veterans. The association's mission is "to ensure that future generations have an organization that is dedicated to keeping this important history alive and to honor its fallen."[6]

CHAPTER 10

Two Medal of Honor Recipients, Two Different Stories

I had an unusual experience in Frankenburg, where all available hands were pressed into service processing the droves of surrendering Germans. Searching one man, a perfect example of the Aryan youth of Hitler's dreams, I found a pistol strapped to the inside of one of his legs. In perfect Oxford English (he later told me he had been educated in England), he said, "Look at that gun!" I did, and on the barrel read "Smith & Wesson, U.S. Government Property." "O.K., what's the story?" I asked. He fired back, "My father took that from an American prisoner in World War I." He paused for a moment, then said reflectively, "You know, we don't solve international problems with war! We just end up trading weapons!"

—Forrest J. Robinson, 104th Military Police Platoon

Two men of the 104th Timberwolf Division distinguished themselves beyond all others during World War II. One was Cecil H. Bolton, the commander of the weapons platoon of Company E, 413th Infantry. The other was Private First Class Willy F. James Jr., lead scout for Company G, 413th Infantry. Each was awarded the Medal of Honor.

Recognition for Cecil Bolton came quickly. Full recognition for Willy James, an African American, came a half century later.

CECIL BOLTON

Cecil Hamilton Bolton was born October 7, 1908, in Crawfordville, Florida. He married Babette De Fronch of Louisville, Kentucky, in 1934.[1] She died in 1939. He married Bessie Mabel McNabb in 1939. He was 32 when he registered for the draft in Huntsville, Alabama, on October 16, 1940, and entered Army service July 27, 1942, at Fort McClellan, Alabama. He attended officer candidate school at Fort Benning, Georgia, and was commissioned a Second Lieutenant. He was sent overseas with an assignment as Weapons Platoon Leader of Company E.

It was easy to imagine that Bolton would be a leader of men. He was nearly six feet tall, weighed 220 pounds, and had been a prizefighter before the war. On the night of November 2, 1944, he took part in an assault by his company after a crossing of the Mark River in Holland. As a First Lieutenant he was the leader of the weapons platoon of Company E. His Medal of Honor citation signed by President Harry S. Truman records extraordinary heroism.

When two machine guns pinned down his company, he tried to eliminate, with mortar fire, their grazing fire which was inflicting serious casualties and preventing the company's advance from an area rocked by artillery shelling. In the moonlight it was impossible for him to locate accurately the enemy's camouflaged positions; but he continued to direct fire until wounded severely in the legs and rendered unconscious by a German shell. When he recovered consciousness, he instructed his unit and then crawled to the forward rifle platoon positions. Taking a two-man bazooka team on his voluntary mission, he advanced chest-deep in chilling water along a canal toward one enemy machine gun. While the bazooka team covered him, he approached alone to within 15 yards of the hostile emplacement in a house. He charged the remaining distance and killed the two gunners with hand grenades. Returning to his men he led them through intense fire over open ground to assault the second German machine gun. An enemy sniper who tried to block the way was dispatched, and the trio pressed on. When discovered by the machine-gun crew and subjected to direct fire 1st Lt. Bolton killed one of the three gunners with carbine fire, and his two comrades shot the others. Continuing to disregard his wounds he led the bazooka team toward an 88-mm artillery piece which was having telling effect on the American ranks, and approached once more through icy canal water until he could dimly make out the gun's silhouette. Under his fire direction, the two soldiers knocked out the enemy weapon with rockets. On the way back to his own lines he was again wounded. To prevent his men being longer subjected to deadly fire, he refused aid and ordered them back to safety, painfully crawling after them until he reached his lines, where he collapsed. First Lt. Bolton's heroic assaults in the face of vicious fire, his inspiring leadership and continued aggressiveness even though suffering from serious wounds, contributed in large measure to overcoming strong enemy resistance and made it possible for his battalion to reach its objective.[2]

After World War II Bolton remained on active duty with service in the Korean War. He retired as a colonel. In addition to the Medal of Honor, he received the Silver Star, two Bronze Stars, the Army Commendation Medal, and the Purple Heart with multiple Oak Leaf Clusters.[3] He died January 22, 1965, at Brooke Army Hospital in San Antonio and is buried at the Fort Sam Houston Military Cemetery with his second wife, Bessie. She died April 3, 1978.

WILLY F. JAMES JR.

Willy Frederick James Jr. was born March 18, 1920, in Kansas City, Missouri, and was 21 years old when he registered for the draft July 1, 1941, at the Municipal Auditorium in Kansas City. He gave his occupation as delivery boy for Crown Drug Co. in the city. He stood 5 feet, 7 inches tall and weighed 143 pounds.[4] He was married to Valcenie James when he entered service in September 1942. After being shipped overseas, James volunteered for frontline duty and was among 2,200 Black soldiers selected to train as combat infantry. This reversed an unwritten Army policy which had largely stopped African American soldiers from joining combat units. He emerged from a four-week training course with distinction and a promotion to Private First Class. His duty assignment was as a scout with the 413th Infantry Regiment of the Timberwolf Division.[5]

On April 7, 1945, James' unit crossed the Weser River near Lippoldsberg, Germany. James went forward to scout the German position but was pinned down by heavy fire. He managed to get back to his company and report what he had seen. A World War II Museum article reported:

James volunteered to lead the attack on Lippoldsberg. As the men advanced, they drew fire from every direction. SS troops emerged from the windows and doorways of the town. Platoon leader, Lieutenant A. J. Serabella was gravely wounded in the attack.[6] James raced to his aid, intending to pull him to safety. Before he could make any movements, James was struck and killed by German sniper fire.[7]

His Medal of Honor citation noted:

> Private First Class James' extraordinary heroic action in the face of withering enemy fire provided the disposition of enemy troops to his platoon. Inspired to the utmost by Private First Class James' self-sacrifice, the platoon sustained the momentum of the assault and successfully accomplished its mission with a minimum of casualties. Private First Class James contributed very definitely to the success of his battalion in the vitally important combat operation of establishing and expanding a bridgehead over the Weser River. His fearless, self-assigned actions, far above and beyond the normal call of duty, exemplify the finest traditions of the American combat soldier and reflect with highest credit upon Private First Class James and the Armed Forces of the United States.[8]

James's heroism was recognized with the nation's second highest award for valor, the Distinguished Service Cross. The award was sent to his 25-year-old widow in September 1945. The World War II Museum article noted: "Not a single photograph of James existed so Valcenie commissioned a portrait of her husband as a way to remember him."

The elevation of James and six other Black World War II service members to receive the Medal of Honor came only after Secretary of the Army John Shannon commissioned in 1993 an academic study to determine why none of the 433 Medals of Honor awarded during World War II went to Black service members. The commission report titled *The Exclusion of Black Soldiers from the Medal of Honor in World War II* documented the denial of the Medal of Honor for deserving Black soldiers during the war.[9]

In 1993 President Bill Clinton asked Congress to extend the amount of time to award the Medal of Honor for seven Black service members. And

at a January 13, 1997, ceremony at the White House, the seven were honored by President Clinton. Only one recipient, Lieutenant Vernon Baker,
attended; the others had passed away and were represented by family
members. President Clinton remarked:

> No African-American who deserved the Medal of Honor for
> his service in World War II received it. Today we fill the gap
> in that picture and give a group of heroes, who also love peace
> but adapted themselves to war, the tribute that has always been
> their due. Now and forever, the truth will be known about these
> African-Americans who gave so much that the rest of us might be
> free.[10]

The seven men honored were Lieutenant Vernon Baker (St. Maries,
Idaho, and Clarinda Iowa), Staff Sergeant Edward A. Carter Jr. (Los Angeles, California), Lieutenant John Fox (Cincinnati, Ohio), Private First Class
Willy James (Kansas City, Missouri), Sergeant Ruben Rivers (Hotulka,
Oklahoma), Lieutenant Charles Thomas (Detroit), and Private George
Watson (Birmingham, Alabama). The *Omaha World Herald* pointed out
that "Although 1.2 million black Americans served in the military during World War II, none was among the 433 recipients of Medals of Honor
awarded in the conflict."[11]

Private First Class Willy James never returned home. He is buried
in Plot P Row 9, Grave 9 at the Netherlands American Cemetery in Margraten. In the summer of 1997, in the presence of his family, a changing-out
ceremony was held to present his new grave marker. The white marble
headstone was engraved with gold-gilded lettering used only to denote
Medal of Honor recipients. Willy F. James Jr. then joined five other Medal
of Honor recipients at Margraten: Lieutenant Colonel Robert Cole (Texas),
502nd Parachute Infantry Regiment 101st Airborne Division; Private
George J. Peters (Rhode Island), 507th Parachute Infantry Regiment; Staff
Sergeant George Peterson (New York), 18th Infantry Regiment, 1st Infantry Division; Private First Class Walter Wetzel (Michigan), 13th Infantry
Regiment, 8th Infantry Division; and First Lieutenant Walter J. Will (New
York), 18th Infantry Regiment, 1st Infantry Division.[12]

The integration of 2,000 Black soldiers into white units at the time of
the Battle of the Bulge was the response to a battlefield manpower shortage

Figure 26. Grave marker of Medal of Honor recipient Willy James. Photo courtesy American Battle Monuments Commission.

and not a policy decision on ending the separation of the races within the Armed Forces. There were already predominantly African American units in World War II in the Atlantic and Pacific theaters to include combat units. Americans are probably most familiar with the example of the Tuskegee Airmen.

The real end to segregation in the military began when President Harry Truman signed Executive Order 9981 on July 26, 1948, directing the Armed Forces to treat all service members equally without regard to race, color, religion, or national origin. This provided the administrative basis for integrating the Armed Forces. And it was another forty-nine years before James and his fellow African American service members were given full recognition for their acts of selfless heroism.

There is an additional note to add to the story of Private First Class Willy James. A former US Marine, retired First Sergeant Robert Gray III, has sought for the last two decades to bring recognition to James. Gray, who like James, is from Kansas City, said: "When I started asking around in 2006 about PFC James, I found there was nothing in Kansas City named after him. No one knew his story. No one knew that he was a Medal of

Honor recipient. I wanted to know where his medal was displayed. There had been no recognition in 1997 when the medal was brought back to St. Louis and no plan to display it. Finally, I found that it was being kept by the niece of Valcenie James and that it had been loaned out to the World War II Museum as a part of the 'Fighting for the Right to Fight' exhibit."

Gray said he assisted the family in getting the medal returned to Kansas City in 2023 and paid for the display in which it now rests in the Black Archives of Mid-America in Kansas City. Gray now sponsors a special ceremony every year to honor James around March 25, which is National Medal of Honor Recognition Day. "This is where Willy James lived," Gray said. "His widow is buried right here at the Army National Cemetery in Ft. Leavenworth. We need to name a statue for him or put something in place and get the city to recognize this African American's sacrifice."[13]

CHAPTER 11

James Gibson and the House on Averette Street

The cottage I call the Blanton house on the back street in Nichols is still there. However, the original families from the neighborhood are all gone, most of them buried over the past half century at Riverside Cemetery across the Lumber River in Horry County. The big Worth Norman garage behind the Blanton house along Highway 76 no longer exists. The once beautiful Gilmore home on the same block is still there, a bit worse for the wear. Dr. Harold Gilmore and his wife Janice are among those who rest eternally at Riverside. Across the road from my grandmother's old home, the faded red-brick C. E. Connelly general store is a forlorn, empty shell. My father's sister Miriam, her husband Sonny Connelly, and their children, my cousins Carolyn, Jimmy, and Gene are gone, all of them only memories to be visited at Riverside and elsewhere.

I don't regard the other old buildings in our town in the same way I do the little cottage on the back street. That building was once the center of the universe for my family. That changed after the war when my grandmother moved to a new rental home at the east end of town. I am certain escaping the memories of her son's death had something to do with the move.

When she moved out, the Blanton house became the Gibson House, the place where Noah and Bertha Gibson raised their eight daughters and only son, James, born in 1947. Of the Gibsons, I still have contact with their daughter Barbara, a high school friend. But when I think about her, it is not her vivacious, friendly personality that draws a picture in my mind. Instead, the angular face of her brother James flashes in front of my eyes.

"He and I were only one year apart," Barbara Gibson recalled. "We grew up like twins. He always called me Sis. I called him James. We didn't fight. We played together and built forts in the swamp across from our house with the local children. He was a Cub Scout and a Boy Scout in Nichols. He graduated from Mullins High School in 1966, two years after me and was in a technical school in Charleston in 1968. He got along good with his friends and his cousin John Lehto. He was just a good brother. And he did not live a sheltered life. He was the only son and I don't think they would have taken him for Vietnam. But he volunteered for the military. He signed up. He took his training at Fort McClellan in Alabama, I think, and when he got ready to go to Vietnam he spent his last three days at home with me in Atlanta. The time went by so fast it seemed like snapping your finger and he was gone. I never saw him again."

James Donald Gibson, born October 23, 1947, joined the US Army on June 3, 1968, and trained as a combat infantryman like my uncle. He was assigned to the 196th Light Infantry Brigade of the Americal Division in South Vietnam. And there in Quang Tri province on Sunday July 27, 1969, he was killed in combat by small arms fire.[1]

At the time of his death, Specialist Fourth Class James Gibson was four months short of his 22nd birthday and of his rotation date to return home from a one-year tour of duty in Vietnam.

By the time James was killed, the Defense Department had long since changed its World War II procedure from the telegram notice of a service member's death to a visit from casualty assistance officers. And during the Vietnam War years the appearance of a military sedan driving up to a home with a somber pair of uniformed servicemen on board became a familiar, sad, and not infrequent event across the United States. Eventually, more than 58,000 families received such a visit.

Barbara Gibson was married and in Atlanta when her parents were informed of her brother's death. "The Army came and told them," she said. "Nobody in my family ever talked about it with each other. And to this day nobody still says anything."

There was little wait for James's body to be brought home. The military had refined that process also. His remains were at Cox-Collins Funeral Home in Mullins within a week and the funeral service was held at Nichols Baptist Church with burial at Riverside Cemetery on Sunday August 10, 1969.[2]

"His death was devastating, it still is," Barbara Gibson concluded. "There is no other word that can describe it."[3]

When I think about James Gibson and his family and the impact of a military death on a local community, I am reminded of 1994, when, in preparation for a D-Day 50th anniversary edition of *Stars and Stripes*, I assigned a reporter to do a story on the town of Bedford, Virginia and the tragedy its townspeople endured in the days after June 6, 1944. Bedford is home to the National D-Day Memorial and the memorial website gives the story of The Bedford Boys. It notes: "Among the hundreds of thousands of service members waiting off Omaha Beach in Normandy in the pre-dawn hours of June 6, there were forty-four soldiers, sailors, and airmen from the town and surrounding Bedford County. Thirty-seven of the young men were in Company A of the 116th Infantry Regiment of the 29th Division. They were to go ashore in the first wave at Omaha in what would be for nearly all of them their first time in combat. It would also be the only time in combat for nearly half of them. In a few dizzying hours, twenty of the young men from Bedford were dead, several more wounded, and three missing. And in a few days the telegrams from the War Department began to arrive in Bedford, throwing the people of the little town and outlying county into shock. Eventually, when the full total of war dead was revealed, Bedford had the highest per capita loss of service members of any town in the United States."[4]

At the time Bedford had a population of about 3,200 and the county population was less than 30,000.[5] The events are described in Alex Kershaw's 2004 book, *The Bedford Boys*.

During the Vietnam War, families feared the arrival of a military sedan carrying a casualty assistance officer. In thousands of cities and towns across the country, that officer brought the worst news a military family can get, the same death notice that Barbara Gibson's family received. And in a little town like Nichols, practically everyone knew within hours.

As I have wondered about who now remembers my uncle and the young men from our area who died in World War II, I have the same thought about James Gibson. His sister and her remaining family will always remember him. I remember him, mostly because of the irony that the house on the back street in Nichols was the place where the Blantons and then the Gibsons got the awful news that a son had been killed in war.

James Gibson's faded bronze marker on red stone at Riverside Cemetery is there near the graves of his parents and other family members.

I drove out to the cemetery one afternoon just to visit with him. Standing there, I remembered all those years ago talking to him. I recalled his friendship with my cousin Gene Connelly and James's cousin John Lehto. However, those thoughts for me are mostly fading recollections. I am sad that my memory of him slowly dims, for it is the duty of the American Legion, of which I am a part, to always remember. There are more than 58,000 other grave markers spread across the length and breadth of our country from James Gibson's War. Somehow, we must find a way to remember and honor them all.

CHAPTER 12

The Names on a Flag

When the war ended near the Mulde River, the Division Headquarters had been established in a chocolate factory in the village of Delitzsch, Germany. Being in the MP Platoon, our duties were quite far reaching, including that of security for the village. Suddenly on 8 May at about 9:00 a.m., church bells which hadn't rung for years began to ring wildly. Although I was again CQ (Charge of Quarters) at the time, I had to find out what was happening—of course hoping desperately that the bells were heralding the end of the war. I ran out the door, to hear the loud speaker coming from an artillery plane low overhead, announcing the war's end.

As I walked out to the street, suddenly a German soldier appeared out of a door on the other side. It was a fiercely strange moment as we eyeballed each other, and then, almost as if on cue, we both walked to the center of the street and turned to walk the several blocks down hill to the church. Crowds seemingly from every nation represented on German soil that day, came surging from every street toward the church. As our crowd got there, the church was already filled, so it became a huge throng surrounding it.

Suddenly, the old organist whom Dick Wray and I had met the previous day pulled open all the stops on the organ and through the open windows there came the exhilarating strains of Martin Luther's "A Mighty Fortress Is Our God." For all it was an overwhelming moment as when a vast number of the crowd sang that great hymn in their own tongue. Probably this had as much as anything to do with my eventual entry into the ministry.

—*Forrest J. Robinson, 104th Military Police Platoon*

In March 2023 I thought the sentimental, often sad journey with my uncle, the Timberwolf I never met, was nearing the end. Then came a message from Kellie Wallace of Clayton, Georgia, and the research began again, spinning off in an unexpected direction. Kellie responded to a query concerning her grandmother, Mrs. J. H. Atkins, the woman from Landrum, South Carolina, who had written my grandmother a sympathy note in January 1945. Mrs. Atkins wrote that her son Cecil had been present the morning Bud Blanton was killed.

Kellie Wallace wrote: "I have a handful of photos of the concentration camps that no one has probably ever seen. I have Timberwolf patches, a Belgian pistol, and a captured Nazi flag signed by many of the soldiers in Company D, 413 Infantry Regiment, 104th Infantry Division. I may have a few photos of my grandfather and some of his war buddies."

Not long afterward I received from Kellie a digital photograph of the flag, a swastika with names and addresses of Company D soldiers written mostly in haphazard fashion amid all the openings of the broken swastika arms. This collection of signatures almost certainly included some of the young men who had been closest to my uncle. Altogether there were thirty-four signatures. Neither my uncle nor Kellie's grandfather Cecil Atkins had signed, but I knew immediately it was authentic because William Bishop of Taylors was there. And Jack Belcher of Wellford, 32 other men's names, many of them listed on a 104th Infantry D Company roster Kellie had obtained from the Timberwolf archives.

The signatures represented men who reached across a seventy-eight-year chasm of history. Immediately, I wanted to know the rest of them them in the same way I had come to know Willie Bishop and Jack Belcher. The lives behind the signatures were yet another unexplored part of my uncle's history and mine.

These men represented the 104th Infantry, the Timberwolf Division that had fought its way across northern Europe. They had helped close the Ruhr pocket and seen the horror of the Nordhausen concentration camp. They were present at the final destruction of Adolf Hitler's Thousand Year

Figure 27. Cecil Atkins's flag with signature of Willie Bishop and other members of the Timberwolf Division. Photo courtesy Kellie Wallace.

Reich. These were men who joyfully met and drank with the Russians to mark the end of their war. Men who had lived the history I had only experienced in reading books and visiting battle sites.

I resolved to follow the same journey with them I had taken with my uncle. I would attempt to learn what I could about each of them in life and in death. From where had these citizen soldiers come? Big city or small town? Most of the signatures answered that with the addresses they included. Were they high school or college graduates or mostly somewhere in between? Farm smart or city wise? And was anyone who had signed the flag still alive? If so, he would have been almost 100. And what of their lives after the Army? And, finally, where were they buried? Had obituaries been printed that reflected their service with the Timberwolf Division?

I thought it would be mostly an electronic journey, a search of internet records, a survey of Ancestry.com and Find a Grave and Newspapers.com and other online sources. And it was that. But for a few of the men the search yielded a great deal more.

The men on the flag from Company D were among the 16 million Americans who went to war and signed control of their lives away for the duration of the conflict plus six months. There were, undoubtedly, countless others like me, my aunt Betty Mincey, my cousin Charles, Kellie Wallace, Wendy Batey, Kim Patterson, Betty Ray, Frankie Blanton, and Brittie Strickland who remembered them.

I started by making an alphabetical listing of the men who signed the flag. I added to the list Cecil Atkins, the D Company soldier from Landrum, South Carolina, who had come home with the flag bearing all the signatures. The signatures and printed names on the flag represented California, Connecticut, Georgia, Illinois, Indiana, Kentucky, Maryland, North Carolina, New Jersey, New York, South Carolina, Tennessee, Texas, Vermont, Virginia and Washington.

Here is what I found about the individuals who signed the flag and Cecil Atkins, the soldier who brought the flag home:

H. G. ADKINS JR.

Herman Guy Adkins Jr. was born September 29, 1920, at Rock Hill, South Carolina. He was living at home with his parents and two brothers, William (13) and Murray (7) and sister Helen (16) at the time of the 1940 census.[1] He registered for the draft February 16, 1942, and gave his wife, Hannah C. Adkins, as his primary contact.[2] He worked at Rock Hill Finishing and Printing Company before entering the Army on May 28, 1944, and was discharged from service on February 2, 1946. The Chicago and North Western Railroad Company listed him as a truck driver on its employee roll effective October 1949.[3] In the 1950 census, H. G. Adkin Jr. of South Carolina was listed as a Chicago resident with employment as a car polisher at a used car lot. Presumably, the letter s in Adkins was inadvertently dropped by the census taker.[4] He died in Rock Hill on October 7, 1972, at the age of 52.[5] There was no mention of his military service in his obituary, but his grave marker includes the inscription "PFC 413 Infantry." He is buried in Grandview Memorial Park, Rock Hill. Hannah Curry Reid, who was married to the late H. G. Jr. and also to Robert A. Reid, died May 17, 2010, in Rock Hill. She is buried at Old Providence Cemetery in Hogansville, Georgia.[6]

Herman G. Adkins Sr., father of H. G. Adkins, was a World War I veteran and recipient of the Purple Heart. He died at the age of 91 on June 26, 1990.[7] And William (Bill) Franklin Adkins, brother of H. G. Jr., was a US Navy sailor credited with saving the lives of many fellow sailors after PT-79, on which he served as a gunner's mate, was sunk off the island of Luzon in the Philippines on January 31, 1945. He was 18 at the time. Bill Adkins died March 9, 2013, and is buried at Grandview Memorial Park.

PAUL S. ALLEN

Paul Singleton Allen was born August 17, 1924, in Demorest, Georgia.[8] He joined the Army May 29, 1944, at Fort McPherson, Georgia, and was a Company D Timberwolf. His son, 68-year-old Warren Wayne Allen, today lives in the same house in Demorest his father returned to after the war.

"He never said nothing much about the war until a few years before he passed away in 2016," Wayne Allen said.[9] "He went to a Timberwolf reunion one time in Atlanta. And he wanted to see someone he knew in South Carolina. He didn't find them. I found the paper with their names on it. They were Willie Bishop and Jack Belcher. Their names are on the flag he signed."

Paul Allen, a blond-haired, blue-eyed small town Georgia boy with barely a grammar school education, was decorated multiple times for heroism. Among the stack of papers his son kept from his father's wartime service is a wrinkled citation: the Bronze Star with two clusters for repeated heroism. The citation reads: "for heroic achievement in connection with military operations in Germany on 30 March 1945. With utter disregard for his personal safety, Private Allen volunteered for a hazardous patrol through hostile territory. Courageously exposing himself to intense enemy fire, he effectively covered the withdrawal of his patrol so that it could return to his unit with invaluable information. His outstanding heroism, above and beyond the call of duty, exemplifies the finest traditions of the American combat soldier and reflects highest credit upon himself and the armed forces of the United States."[10]

Wayne Allen said four of his father's five brothers served in World War II. "One of them, Robert, was killed in Europe," he said. "He was in the Battle of the Hedge Rows in Normandy and a friendly bomb drifted down on him and he was killed. Robert Allen is buried at Amos Creek Baptist Church in Habersham County."

After the war Paul Allen waited for Emma Belle Williams to finish high school in Clarksville, Georgia, and then married her. He received Veterans Administration training on how to make brooms and did that for many years. He later worked in a textile mill. The couple had two sons, Dennis Allen (1951) and Walter Wayne (1955). Emma Allen died in 2007.[11] Paul died in 2016.[12] They are buried in the Cool Spring United Methodist Church Cemetery in Clarksville, Georgia.

Wayne Allen remembered three things vividly from the few times his father talked about the war: "He said when we came home they had parades, they were celebrating. He didn't understand why they came back from Vietnam and they got nothing."

"And I know from listening to him that it is hard to believe that somebody who is 20 or 21 years old has seen all that. I was going to join the Army and daddy had tears in his eyes. He said that he had seen enough and he didn't want me to do it."

The final thing, Wayne Allen recalled, was the lasting effect the war had on his father: "Daddy had gone to a local preacher to tell him about something that had happened in the war. He said he told the preacher that he was in the Battle of the Bulge and the German tanks were going by their foxholes and shooting everyone in the foxholes as they passed. When they got to him in his foxhole a German soldier pointed his gun at him and it clicked, so he shot the German. It was something he didn't want to talk about. That was right before he passed away." The life and death combat scene Paul Allen apparently had played over and over in his mind since the war had taken place seventy years earlier.

CECIL ATKINS

William Cecil Atkins of Landrum, South Carolina, is the D Company soldier who brought the flag with the signatures home from World War II. His mother, Nora Atkins, wrote my grandmother a sympathy note saying that her son had been present the morning Fletcher Blanton was killed. And it was his granddaughter, Kellie Wallace of Clayton, Georgia, who sent me photographs of the captured flag with the signatures.[13]

Kellie's grandfather Cecil was born February 8, 1920, at Landrum in Spartanburg County, South Carolina. In the 1940 census he was listed as a family member in the household of John H. Atkins, superintendent at Damask Mill. Cecil, 20, was a dryer at the mill. The Atkins household included his mother Nora plus his brother John H. Atkins Jr. (17) and sisters Aileen (13), Louise (9), and Lucile (9).[14] On his draft registration dated June 28, 1942, Cecil listed his father J. H. Atkins as his primary contact. His employer was Drayton Mills in Drayton, South Carolina, also in Spartanburg County.[15] He joined the Army on May 31, 1944, at Fort Bragg. His separation date from the military was not available, nor was information on his marriage to Ruth Daniel.[16]

In the 1950 census 30-year-old William Cecil Atkins was the head of household with his wife Ruth and son Richard (9) living in the small town of Campobello, about fifteen miles northwest of Spartanburg. His occupation was listed as machine operator in a local mill.[17] At the time of his death September 1, 1976, he was the weaving superintendent for Brookline Carpet in Greenville, South Carolina.[18] He is buried in Evergreen Memorial Gardens in Landrum. Ruth Daniel Atkins died May 14, 2014, at age 94. Cecil and Ruth's only son, Richard Alvin Atkins, father of Kellie Wallace, died January 3 of the same year. Kellie Wallace said, "We don't think she (her grandmother) knew that he passed away first and were grateful for that at the time."

HOWARD BAILEY

Howard Ray Bailey gave his address as 1400 Asheboro Street, Greensboro, North Carolina, when he signed the German flag with other Company D members. Howard was born February 4, 1920, to Bud and Minnie Bailey, and the family resided at 603 Union Street in Greensboro during the 1930 census.[19] He married Lillie May Thomas of Danville, Virginia, on June 30, 1940, and registered for the draft in July 1941, listing his occupation as paper hanger.[20] He enlisted May 29, 1944, at Fort Bragg and served until November 11, 1945. On the 1950 census he was the head of a household that included his wife Lillie, a daughter, Sharon (8), and sons Howard M. (6) and Ronald (3). His 72-year-old father was also a household member. He listed his occupation as route driver for a commercial laundry. His wife

Lillie died in 1980 and he died December 23, 1992, and is buried at Forest Lawn Cemetery in Greensboro. His grave marker shows his PFC rank and World War II Army service.

JACK BELCHER

Jack Belcher was born June 3, 1920, in Valley Falls, South Carolina, near Spartanburg and was 21 years old when he registered for the draft June 20, 1941. He listed his primary contact as his wife Annie Lou Hawkins Belcher of Wellford, South Carolina. His occupation was listed as weaver working for the Jackson Mill at Wellford.[21] He enlisted May 30, 1944, at Fort Bragg. After the war he resumed work in the textile industry and was a longtime Textile League baseball player. He died November 17, 1994, in Spartanburg and is buried at Wood Memorial Park in Greenville.[22]

WILLIAM M. BISHOP

As noted earlier (Chapter 3), Willie Bishop was one of three service members who visited my grandmother in 1945 after her son Fletcher Blanton's death. Willie was born William Manley Bishop on March 20, 1920, in Greenville County, South Carolina. He married Helen Julia Fleming on October 16, 1937. In the 1940 census, he and Helen lived in Taylors and he worked in textiles at the Southern Bleachery.[23] He was 21 when he registered for the draft June 21, 1941, listing Helen as his primary contact and his employment as a textile worker at Southern Bleachery and Printworks in Taylors.[24] Willie became a lifelong friend to the Blanton family. He died January 4, 2007, and is buried at Woodlawn Memorial Park Mausoleum in Greenville, South Carolina.

THOMAS BLACKWELL

Thomas Marion Blackwell was born April 15, 1919, in Rutherford County, North Carolina. He was 21 and living on Rural Route 3 in Gaffney, South Carolina, when he registered for the draft October 16, 1940, listing his mother Della Blackwell Amos as his primary contact. He had a job at the Gaffney Manufacturing Co.[25] His enlistment date was May 31, 1944, at Fort Bragg, North Carolina. After leaving service he married Julia Mae Mc-Craw. On the 1950 census he was head of household with his wife and a seven-year-old daughter. He listed cotton mill worker as his employment.[26]

Julia Mae Blackwell died August 9, 1966, and Thomas was 89 when he died November 24, 2008. They are buried at Springhill Memorial Gardens in Chesnee, South Carolina.

LEO V. BLOOM

Leo Victor Bloom was born March 30, 1923, in Baltimore, Maryland. He listed his mother, Rose Bloom of 2535 Boarman Avenue, as his primary contact on his draft registration form completed June 30, 1942. His employer was Bloom Brothers Photographers at the same address.[27] He entered Army service March 9, 1943, at Baltimore and was discharged November 21, 1945.[28] In earlier research of the soldiers who signed the flag, Kellie Wallace, granddaughter of Cecil Atkins, said that a cousin of Leo Bloom confirmed that Leo had been a medic with the regiment when he signed the flag. Leo Bloom married Annette Malchowsky on July 19, 1945.[29]

Leo and two brothers operated a photo processing company, Paramount Photo Service, Inc., after World War II. A *Baltimore Sun* article reported that he and a brother started the company while he was a student at Baltimore City College, and after the war they revived the business. He died July 28, 1982, at the age of 59.[30] Annette Bloom Samuels died February 17, 2017.[31]

RAY J. BROWN

The search for Ray J. Brown was more complicated that for most of the other men. William Ray Brown was also from Hammond and a WWII veteran and Purple heart recipient. But the only draft board registrant in Hammond to exactly fit the signature was Ray John Brown. He was 23 when he signed up for the draft Oct. 16, 1940. His employer was Inland Steel Co., in Indiana Harbor in his home county of Lake.[32] His military enlistment information showed he joined the Army Jan. 21, 1943, at Indianapolis.[33] Ray was listed as a sergeant on an unofficial Company D roster obtained by Kellie Wallace. On the 1950 census he listed his occupation as railroad switchman at a steel mill. He was the head of household with two children, Teresa (2) and Bruce (1) His wife was Hertha C. Brown.[34] His obituary noted, "On Oct. 21, 1946, in Valparaiso, he married Hertha Larsen, who preceded him in death in 1962." Ray died June 22, 1972 and special services were conducted by the Wheatfield American Legion Post

406 where he was a member.[35] He is buried at Chapel Lawn Memorial Gardens, Schererville, Indiana.

WILFRED CAMPBELL

Wilfred Howerton Campbell was born June 10, 1920, in Evansville, Indiana. He was 21 when he registered for the draft, listing his mother Opel A. Campbell as his primary contact. He was a truck driver for Red Arrow Delivery in Evansville.[36] He entered service July 19, 1944, and was discharged January 22, 1946.[37] After the war he married Ethel Alvira Stephens. In the 1950 census he was listed as head of household in Denver, Colorado, along with his wife Ethel and sons James C. (2) and Stephen W., an infant. He listed his occupation as shipping clerk in a meat packing plant.

Wilfred, 60, died of a heart attack September 20, 1980, in Denver and is buried at Fort Logan National Cemetery in Denver.[38] Ethel died October 30, 2004, and is buried with her husband at the national cemetery.[39]

BILL CARRIGAN

Billy Lee Carrigan was born August 5, 1921, at Taylorsville, North Carolina. He was 20 when he registered for the draft at the Alexander County Local Board number 1 on February 16, 1942. He listed Miss Stella Kerley of Taylorsville as his primary contact.[40] Bill entered service September 2, 1942, and began active duty two weeks later. He was discharged January 22, 1946, with the rank of Technician Fifth Grade. He was overseas for sixteen months of that time.[41]

After the war he was a furniture worker. He married Lucille Harris of Taylorsville on December 1, 1950.[42] At the time of his death at age 53 (October 14, 1974), his survivors included his wife Lucille and two children, a son Wayne Carrigan of Gadsden, Alabama, and daughter Jill Carrigan of the family home.[43] He is buried at the Taylorsville City Cemetery.

Bill Carrigan's younger brother, 21-year-old Army private James Robert Carrigan, was killed in action January 1, 1945, in Belgium during the Battle of the Bulge. He is also buried at the Taylorsville City Cemetery.

ROY CLEMENTS

James Roy Clements was born July 19, 1924, in Casey County, Kentucky. He was a student at Clementsville High when he registered for the draft. He listed his father Lambert as his primary contact.[44] He entered service July 19, 1944, and was discharged December 19, 1946.[45] After his military service, he returned to farm work and was listed on the 1950 census as a helper for his father.[46] He married Mary Elizabeth Payne on October 13, 1952, then rejoined the Army on September 30, 1953. He retired from service December 31, 1968, as a 1st Sergeant. His newspaper obituary notes that he worked for US Steel after his last stint of Army service. He died July 31, 1977, at the age of 53. His gravestone inscription shows service in World War II and in Korea. According to his grave information file, he left behind his wife and three sisters, Helen Goode of Liberty (Kentucky), Josephine Wethington of Lebanon, Indiana, and Kathlene Grooms of Marcelles, Illinois.[47] Mary Elizabeth Clements, 66, died September 2, 1990. No children were listed in her obituary.[48] The couple are buried at Saint Bernard Cemetery in Clementsville.

NEWTON H. CORBITT

Newton Hunter Corbitt was born September 1, 1923. In the 1940 census he listed himself as a day laborer living with his family in Williamson County, Tennessee. His father worked at a local sawmill. Newton joined the Army at Camp Forrest, Tennessee, on November 10, 1942. He served three years and was discharged November 28, 1945. In the 1950 census he was listed as head of household in Nashville with wife Margaret, daughter Janice (3), and infant son Calvin. He listed his occupation as worker for a flooring company. He died March 29, 1983.[49] His wife Margaret died Oct. 10, 2009.[50] They are buried at the National Cemetery in Nashville.

GEORGE R. DECKER

George Robert Decker was born June 13, 1923, in Grayson County, Kentucky. The 1940 census listed the Decker household as Leslie Decker, his wife Mallie, and sons Roosevelt, George R., and Herbert. The Deckers had four daughters, Mary, Mildred, Allene, and Alice. George gave his occupation as farm help when he registered for the draft June 30, 1942. He lived on Rural Route 2, Caneyville, Kentucky, and listed his mother Mallie Decker as his primary contact and employer. George entered military service January 31, 1944, and was discharged May 5, 1946. He married Lorene Mudd and in the 1950 census the family also included two daughters,

Diane (4) and Bulah Mae (2). George listed his occupation as farmer.[51] Lorene Decker died February 4, 1994, and George died in Caneyville on October 12, 1994. The Deckers are buried at the Wilson Cemetery in Grayson County, Kentucky.[52]

HAROLD G. EKSTROM

Harold Gust Ekstrom was born March 19, 1916, in Moline, Illinois. He was 24 years old when he registered for the draft October 16, 1940, and was employed at John Deere Plow Works. His father Harold Gust Ekstrom was his primary contact.[53] He entered service December 4, 1942, and was married November 28, 1943, to Juanita Jorns of Chicago. The local newspaper reported that Ekstrom "has been stationed at Camp Adair, Ore., since November 1942, but has been transferred to desert maneuvers near Camp Heider, Ariz. On conclusion of their visit here, Mrs. Ekstrom will return to Chicago where she will remain with her parents for the present and Private Ekstrom will report to his new station."[54]

He was discharged from service December 10, 1945.[55] The 1950 census listed him as head of household with his wife Juanita and son David (2). He was employed in the motor assembly section at a factory. Harold Ekstrom died September 16, 1989, and Juanita Ekstrom died July 6, 1991. She is buried at Fairview Memorial Park Cemetery in Cook County, Illinois, and Harold's grave is thought to be there also.[56]

MILTON FELDMAN

On the flag, Milton Feldman gave the address of 601 West 148th Street, New York, New York. After searching through at least 25 Milton Feldman draft card registrations entries online I found a draft registration card for MILTON FELDMAN of 601 W. 148th St. NYC. Unfortunately, the card was unlike any other I had come across in the draft registration search. It was a single index card with Serial #320 MILTON FELDMAN Order #3865 at the top. Below was typed 10/22/45 601 W. 148 St. NYC. Both parts of the normal draft registration were missing.[57]

Among the possibilities rejected early on before finding the single draft card entry were: Milton Feldman, a 25-year-old Department of Sanitation employee in the Bronx, when he registered for the draft. He struck through his written address of 1937 Davidson Avenue in the Bronx on his draft card.[58] Also there was Milton Feldman of 77 Riverdale Ave. in Brooklyn. He was a student at the College of Dentistry at New York University.[59] There was also Milton Feldman of 280 E. 95th St. in Brooklyn. He was born in 1914 and less likely to be a private in the Timberwolf Division.[60] And Milton Feldman of 2075 E. 16th Street in Brooklyn. He was also born in 1914.[61] Another was Milton Maurice Feldman of Washington Avenue in the city.[62] And another was Milton Feldman of 766 East 53rd Street, Kings, New York.[63]

I continued the search for another day online and found additional Milton Feldman listings. For a while I thought Milton Feldman of Brooklyn (266th Kosciusko Street) was the D Company member. But the single card with Milton Feldman's address from the flag signature eventually ruled out the dozens of other Milton Feldman registrations out. Without further documentation I was unable to track Milton's life further than his draft registration and his signing of the flag.

ERASMO GARZA

Erasmo Garza was born January 25, 1925, in Corpus Christi, Texas.[64] He registered for the draft January 25, 1943, and joined the Army at Fort Sam, Houston, Texas, on October 13, 1943. On his draft registration card he gave his address as 2519 Coleman, the same Corpus Christi address he signed on the flag. He was discharged after fifteen months in service in early 1945 and married Amalia Mendoza on July 22, 1945.[65] In the 1950 census E. Garza listed road construction employment with the Corpus Christi street department. The couple had a one-year-old son, also listed as E. Garza, at the time of the census.[66] His wife died September 25, 1992, and he died March 9, 2003. They are buried at the Oakland Baptist Church Cemetery in Richardsville, Virginia and their single tombstone bears a Purple Heart.

RAYMOND HENKE

The signature on the flag was simply Raymond Henke with no address. The listing on a wartime 413th D Company roster shows Raymond P. Henke. Online, the only draft registration for Raymond P. Henke is for Raymond P. Henke of 70 Wilkes Avenue, Buffalo, New York. Henke was born December 26, 1903, and listed his wife Doris Henke as his primary contact.

He listed his employer as the I.R.C. Railway Co. and Broadway Station as his place of employment. He registered for the draft February 15, 1942, in Buffalo.[67] Raymond Paul Henke had married Doris Elaine Henry in Buffalo on January 2, 1928.[68] In the 1930 census he was head of the household with Doris as the only other family member. He listed his employment as radio serviceman. In the 1940 census he was still listed as a radio serviceman, and the couple had three sons, James (9), Paul (6), and Thomas (1). The usual enlistment information was not available online, but a roster of Company D, 413th Regiment of the 104th Division shows Raymond P. Henke as a private first class.

In the 1950 census Raymond identified himself as a salesman for a retail bakery. He died April 15, 1956, and is buried at Mount Calvary Cemetery in Cheektowaga, New York.[69] Doris Henke remarried and died November 10, 1999. Her obituary noted that she was predeceased by her husbands, Raymond P. Henke and Colonel Joseph S. Snyder. She is also buried in the Mount Calvary cemetery.[70]

J. D. JOHNSON

Joy DeWitt Johnson was born October 26, 1923, in Spencer, Indiana. He was the son of Horace Wesley Johnson and Olive Leona Galimore Johnson of 324 N. Montgomery Street in Spencer. He registered for the draft June 30, 1942, and joined the service March 9, 1943, at Fort Benjamin Harrison, Indiana. He married Olive Ann Arthur of Spencer, Indiana, on July 23, 1945, in Indianapolis and was discharged from service December 15, 1945.[71]

The Johnsons lived in Indianapolis for more than two decades, and Joy Johnson worked as an experimental engineer with Detroit Diesel Allison Division of General Motors. He died June 21, 1980, after suffering a heart attack while riding his bicycle near the town of Plainfield, Indiana. He was 56. Olive Ann died August 11, 2011, at the age of 89.[72]

RAY JOHNSON

Ray Johnson signed the flag with a Poulsbo, Washington, address. My search succeeded fairly quickly when the obituary for Raymond Samuel Johnson, in a Washington state newspaper noted, "In 1941, Ray Johnson traveled from Fort Bliss, Texas to the state of Washington, being attached to the 202nd Coast Artillery after the attack on Pearl Harbor. He was then stationed at Keyport and Lemolo, where he met the love of his life, Doris (Kolstad). The two were married in Poulsbo, Washington. He was then sent to Germany and was assigned to the Timberwolf Division . . . , serving his country during World War II."[73]

Ray Johnson was born Dec. 22, 1918, in Mount Olive, Illinois. He registered for the draft Oct. 16, 1942, at the age of 21. He listed his mother, Mrs. Sam Johnson, as his primary contact and employment at National Ribbon and Carbon in Chicago.[74] He entered service in 1941 at Chicago.[75] His obituary noted that after the war he worked as a planner and estimator for the Department of Defense in Bangor, Washington.

The obituary added, "Papa Ray," as he was affectionately known, is survived by his loving wife of 67 years, Doris, and his children, Karen Johnson, Linda Grebb (Jerry), Carol Pearson (Marc), and Terry Johnson (Kerri); his 7 grandchildren; his 7 great-grandchildren. . . ." He is buried at Tahoma National Cemetery in Kent, Washington, along with Doris who died in 2012.

ALFRED M. LANGBERG

Alfred Merrill Langberg was born March 6, 1923, in Paulsboro, New Jersey. He was 19 when he registered for the draft. He listed his father, Alfred L. Langberg, as his contact at 608 N. Delaware St., Paulsboro. This is the same address he wrote on the captured flag. He signed his draft registration card as A. Merrill Langberg.[76] He was engaged to Hilda Miller in March 1944 and they married July 11, 1945, when he returned from the war.[77] The wedding story reported that Staff Sergeant Langberg "has but recently returned after 10 months' service with the 104th Division of the First Army in Europe and will report to Fort Dix at the end of a 30-day furlough."[78] He began work after the war as a draftsman at the firm Hungerford and Terry, Inc. and later served as chief engineer and then president of the company. He retired in 1996 after forty-eight years with the firm.[79] Alfred Langberg died August 5, 2005. He was 82. Hilda Langberg, 83, died August 23, 2006. They are buried at the Eglington Cemetery, Clarksboro, New Jersey.

CHARLES LASSITER

Charles Herman Lassiter was born February 28, 1918, in Guilford County, North Carolina. He registered for the draft October 16, 1940, and listed his mother, Louella Spivey Lassiter, as his primary contact. He worked at Snow Lumber Company in High Point.[80] His mother was listed as head of the family in the 1940 census when Charles was 22 years old. He joined the Army on November 12, 1942, at Camp Croft, South Carolina,[81] and left service December 7, 1945. In the 1950 census he was listed as head of household and worked at a lumber mill. The other family members were his wife Evelyn, who worked at a hosiery mill, and their sons Jerry (7) and Charles (3).[82] Charles H. Lassiter, 66, died November 27, 1984, and his status was listed as divorced.[83] He was buried at Oakwood Cemetery in High Point.

WILLIAM R. LAWLESS

William Ralph Lawless was born July 10, 1923, to John and Marie Lawless in Anderson County, South Carolina, near the small town of Piedmont. In the 1940 census his mother Marie was listed as the head of household with three of the four Lawless sons still at home.[84] Ralph was 18 when he registered for the draft June 30, 1942.[85] A marriage license was granted to William Ralph Lawless and Doris Virginia Woodcock of nearby Pelzer, South Carolina, on October 19, 1944; he was 21, and she was 18. Ralph Lawless returned to the West Pelzer upstate area after the war. An account of his life noted that he retired from work with Gerber Childrenswear.[86]

One of Ralph and Doris Lawless's sons, William Jr., joined the Army on September 10, 1964. Three years later, on January 8, 1967, Sergeant William R. Lawless Jr., a member of Co. C, 1st Battalion 27th Infantry of the 25th Infantry Division, was killed in action in Vietnam's Binh Duong province.[87]

Ralph Lawless Sr. died April 13, 1999, in Anderson, South Carolina. His obituary noted that he was a US Army veteran. His wife, Doris Virginia Woodcock Lawless, died September 14, 2015.[88] They are buried in Greenville Memorial Gardens, Piedmont, in Greenville County.

BILL LEADLEY

The signature on the flag appears to be written Bill Leadly, not Leadley, and to further confuse things, an Iowa veterans bonus application by Bill Leadley of Fort Dodge listed his unit as D Company, 443rd Infantry, not the 413th. Nevertheless, I believe I found the man who signed the flag.

Billy Dean Leadley was born in Mallard, Iowa, on July 1, 1922, to Percy Calvin Leadley, a farmer, and Stella May Clark Leadley.[89] He registered for the draft June 30, 1942, giving his age as 19 and his home as 1420 3rd Ave. N. in Fort Dodge, the same town written on the captured flag. He attended Fort Dodge High School.[90] His draft registration indicates he was employed at Hutchinson Grocery in Fort Dodge when he registered in June 1942.[91] His application for the Iowa military bonus after the war indicated he entered active duty November 19, 1942, at Camp Dodge, Iowa, and went overseas August 27, 1944. He returned to the US on July 3, 1945, and was discharged from the Army on December 9, 1945.

He married Shirley M. Wienke in February 1948.[92] In the 1950 census he listed his employment as sales and delivery in Fort Dodge.[93] Bill Leadley died April 6, 2010, and is buried in Saint Paul Lutheran Cemetery in Palmer, Iowa, along with his wife Shirley, who died August 21, 2022. There is no mention of military service on the joint grave marker.[94] A gravestone inscription notes "PARENTS OF KATHALENE, MICHELE & LORI."

After pursuing a lead on Facebook for Lori Bauer, believed to be the daughter of Bill Leadley, I received an email from her. "I hear that you are wanting some information on Bill Leadley," she wrote. "What are you looking for? I am one of his daughters." It was signed Lori B. I messaged back three times and had one brief answer but never received any further information on Bill Leadley.

GEORGE MEGARRY

George E. Megarry was born November 25, 1920, in Frankfort, Illinois. He registered for the draft February 16, 1942, at the Chicago Local Board 105 on 153 W. 69th Street, Chicago. He listed his employer as Bruno Kreives-Tavern. His father, George Megarry Sr., was listed as his contact, and the family address was 6319 Parnell Avenue, Chicago.[95] That is the same address he wrote on the captured Nazi flag signed by Company D members. George E. Megarry married June Alma Mathews of Cook County, Illinois, on January 12, 1950.[96] In the 1950 census he was head of household with June and a son, Harry M. (7), as family members. His employment was listed as freight router.[97] Unfortunately, I could not find further information on any of the George E. Megarry family members.

GEORGE P. MEADOWS

George Parker Meadows was born August 25, 1925, at Clifton Forge, Virginia. He registered for the draft on his birthday in 1943 and listed his mother, Blanche Meadows, as his primary contact. He was employed at the Richmond, Fredericksburg and Potomac Railroad Company in Fredericksburg.[98] No record was found of his service dates but after his military discharge he married Edna Heenan of Richmond on December 30, 1948.[99] The couple were both students at Mary Washington College in Fredericksburg at the time of their marriage.[100]

After graduation George Meadows was a high school teacher in the Henrico County (Virginia) schools for thirty years. He taught at Tucker High School and Byrd Middle School, where he was chairman of the history department, a story on his life reported. "Mr. Meadows served during WWII with the 104th Timberwolf Division, 413th Regiment and was awarded the Bronze Star," the *Richmond News Leader* reported.[101] He died April 12, 1995, at the age of 69. Edna Heenan Meadows died January 7, 2014. She was 85.[102] They are buried at Forest Lawn Cemetery in Richmond.

A. J. PETRELLA

Adam John Petrella was born February 20, 1911. He was 29 years old when he registered for the draft October 16, 1940.[103] He had married 21-year-old Avalene Rife of Circleville, Ohio, in February 1934 and was working at Joyce Products in Columbus when he registered. In the 1940 census Adam and Avalene listed a 5-year-old son, James Edward, and a 2-year-old daughter, Joann.

Adam joined the service November 30, 1942, and was discharged September 25, 1945 as a corporal. In the 1950 census he listed his occupation as a railroad switch tender. Avalene Petrella applied for his military grave marker after he died January 11, 1969.[104] And on Line 9 of the military gravestone application was confirmation that he was a member of Co D 413th Infantry, United States Army. Adam, who signed the flag as A.J. Petrella, is buried at St. Joseph Cemetery in Columbus. Avalene Petrella died December 2, 1991.

PAUL SHINKEVICH

Paul Shinkevich was born in Kewanee, Illinois, on August 4, 1912. He was the son of Russian immigrants Mina (Mike) and Stephanie Shinkevich. Four of the Shinkevich sons served in the US military during World War II. Paul registered for the draft October 16, 1940, and listed his home address as 322 E 10th Street, Kewanee.[105] It was the same address he used on the captured flag. He joined the Army on November 21, 1942. His father Mina died in October 1944, most likely while Paul was fighting in Europe. He was discharged from the Army on November 8, 1945. In the 1950 census he was listed as living at home with his mother and his 38-year-old brother.[106] He worked as a machinist for a valve fitting company. He died August 12, 1989, at the age of 77. His obituary noted, "He was a World War II Army veteran, serving as platoon sergeant in the 104th Timberwolf Division. He was awarded the Silver Star for bravery."[107] His nickname with friends was "Snooks" and he was a member of the Veterans of Foreign Wars Post 8078 and the Flemish-American Club.[108] He is buried in South Pleasant View Cemetery, Kewanee, Illinois.

MAURICE SHOEMAKER

Maurice Ryan Shoemaker was born August 28, 1922, and registered for the draft June 30, 1942, at the Logan County local board office in Russellville, Kentucky. His home address was Rural Route 1, Lewisburg and he indicated he worked for his father A. B. Shoemaker, who was a farmer.[109] He entered active service December 1, 1942, and was discharged December 15, 1945.[110] He married Elizabeth Stuart in Lewisburg, Kentucky, on January 3, 1946, and the wedding notice said the couple would live in Birmingham, Alabama, where Maurice would be employed.[111] After the war he joined the American Legion and the Timberwolf Association. He was also a member of the Aluminum Workers Union. In the 1950 census he was listed as head of household in Logan County, Kentucky, along with his wife Elizabeth and their son Jerry (2). His occupation was farmer.[112] He died August 31, 1997, in Jeffersonville, Indiana.[113] The Shoemakers had three sons and a daughter. They were listed as Jerry of Bowling Green, Kentucky,

Ronald of Clarksville, Indiana, and Keith of Jeffersonville, Indiana, plus daughter Pam Shoemaker Abell of New Albany, Indiana. Elizabeth Shoemaker died September 9, 2015. The couple is buried at Stuart Chapel Cemetery, Lewisburg, Kentucky.

L. F. SIMON

Lester Fred Simon was born Christmas Day 1919 in Glencoe, Missouri. He registered for Selective Service on July 1, 1941, and gave his occupation as a laborer.[114] On June 13, 1942, he applied for a marriage license in St. Louis with 19-year-old Ruby Broemmelsick of Glencoe.[115] They were married shortly afterward.[116] On August 15, 1942, he enlisted in the US Army.

As a member of the Timberwolf Division, Lester was wounded in battle in December 1944. Military doctors removed artillery shell fragments from his face, and he was returned to duty.[117] He was awarded the Silver Star for bravery in combat and held the rank of Staff Sergeant at the end of two years and eight months military service. On the 1950 census he listed his occupation as a maintenance man for heating equipment. The Simon family in 1950 included a daughter, Linda (5), and a son, Donald (3).[118]

Lester Simon died at age 80 on July 6, 2000, and is buried with his wife Ruby at Jefferson Barracks National Cemetery in St. Louis.[119] His death notice in the *St. Louis Post-Dispatch* did not mention his military service, although there is an American Flag beside his name.[120] His gravestone, in addition to showing his Purple Heart and Silver Star awards, states, "LOVING HUSBAND DAD AND GRANDPA."[121]

FRANKLIN E. SMITH

Franklin Ernest Smith was born July 2, 1922, in Montesano, Washington. In the 1930 census he was listed as a 7-year-old son in the household headed by Percy Smith who was in the logging business. His mother Mattie and brothers Stanley (5) and Robert (1) were the other members of the household.[122] In the 1940 census he was listed as a 17-year-old son in a household headed by Mattie J. Backland in rural Shelton. Two other brothers were listed, Stanley (16), and Bobby, an infant.[123] At age 19, he still listed his home address as Matlock Route, Shelton, in Mason County Washington on his draft registration card. His primary contact was his mother,

Mattie Backland. He registered for the draft June 30, 1942.[124] He signed the captured flag with his Matlock Route, Shelton address.

Franklin Smith entered military service December 15, 1942, at Tacoma, Washington. He was discharged sometime in 1945 and applied for a marriage license with Louise D. Fish on January 24, 1949, in Lilliwaup, Washington.[125] He listed his address as Lilliwaup in a subsequent public record index.[126] On the 1950 census the Smiths listed an infant daughter, Sandra M. Franklin, and his wife Louise listed their employment as workers at an oyster plant.[127] He died November 9, 1999, in Mason County. The *Olympian* newspaper in Olympia, Washington, reported the death of Sandra Marie (Smith) Young Eberle on November 9, 2015. The obituary noted, "Sandra is preceded in death by her mother, Louise Smith; and her father, Franklin Smith."[128]

RAYMOND T. SUCHOMEL

Raymond Thomas Suchomel was born November 1, 1923, in Cicero, Illinois. He was 18 when he registered for the draft June 27, 1942, and he listed his mother May Suchomel as his primary contact. She lived in the family home at 1817 S. 57th Avenue, Cicero, Illinois. This was the same address he wrote on the flag. He identified his workplace as Electro Motive in La Grange, Illinois, a town outside Chicago.[129] He served from February 24, 1943, until December 8, 1945.[130]

Raymond Suchomel and Mary Ruth Vachout, also of Cicero, married in October 1946. There was no listing for the Suchomels in the 1950 census, but the *Chicago Tribune* and a local funeral home, Hitzeman, noted his death July 3, 2004, at LaGrange Park, Illinois.[131] Mary Ruth Suchomel died April 27, 2013.[132] They are buried at the Queen of Heaven Cemetery in Hillside, Illinois.

JOHN THOMSON

John Stewart Thomson Jr. was born April 5, 1914, in Hartford, Connecticut. He was 26 and married at the time he registered for the draft in 1940. His primary contact was his wife Edith Hall Thomson, who he married in February 1938 in Hartford. He worked for the Connecticut State Highway Department.[133] His enlistment date was February 2, 1944, and he was discharged February 7, 1946.[134] John signed the flag with the home address he listed on his draft registration, 114 Francis Ave. in Hartford.

In the 1950 census he was listed as head of household with Edith and son David (2). He worked as a sign erector for the Connecticut State Highway Department for thirty years before retirement.[135]

Edith Thomson died February 28, 1984. John lived another five years until September 6, 1989. The *Hartford Courant* newspaper reported: "Thompson was a US Army veteran, and was awarded the Bronze Star and the Purple Heart; was Past Commander of May-Davis-Stotzer (American Legion) Post 117." He was survived by a son, David S. Thomson of West Boothbay Harbor, Maine and two grandchildren.[136] John and Edith Thomson are buried at the Evergreen Cemetery in Boothbay, Maine.

BEN F. TRAVIS

Ben F. Travis signed the flag with his name and Los Angeles, Calif as his address. Military records indicate that Benjamin Franklin Travis was born in Delaware, Oklahoma, on Dec. 7, 1923. He registered for the draft at Nowata, Oklahoma, on June 30, 1942. A Los Angeles address, 210 West 115th St., was pencilled at the top of the registration card.[137] Ben enlisted in the Army July 10, 1943, at Los Angeles. He is listed on the 1950 census living in the household of Ben and Etta Travis in Los Angeles and working at a saw mill. California death records show he died Aug. 28, 1990.[138] No further information was available. Another Benjamin Franklin Travis from Onapie, Oklahoma, registered for the draft and served in World War II. But he pencilled a Santa Paula, California, address and not Los Angeles at the top of his draft registration.[139]

JAMES E. WOODHULL

James Edward Woodhull was born September 1, 1913, in Bennington, Vermont. His parents were Joel B. Woodhull and Eliza M. Remington Woodhull of Bennington.[140] He graduated from the University of Vermont in 1937 and enrolled in graduate school at Cornell University in Ithaca, New York. He married Norma Falby of Burlington, Vermont, in June 1940.[141] He registered for the draft October 16, 1940, and listed the town of Derby in Orleans County, Vermont, as his employer.[142]

He entered the Army August 21, 1943, and was discharged November 21, 1945. A published order from 104th Division Headquarters on October 26, 1945, announced that Private First Class James E. Woodhull had been awarded the Bronze Star "for meritorious achievement in connection with military operations in Germany on 22 March 1945."[143]

A Florida government file shows that he was granted a divorce from Norma Falby in 1945.[144] Five years later he married Janice Shively of Burlington, Vermont. He was a state teacher trainer for agricultural education and his wife, a Yale graduate, was an instructor of music at the University of Vermont. Woodhull eventually earned a master's degree in rural education from Cornell University and a doctorate in agricultural education from Pennsylvania State University. He became an official of the Agency for International Development and served in the Philippines, Thailand, and Nigeria. In 1974 he was assigned to Washington, DC, and managed a task force for the resettlement of Vietnamese refugees.[145] He died April 6, 1996, at the age of 82, and his cremated remains are buried at Arlington National Cemetery in the Columbarium (Plot 4M-28–5). Janice Shively Woodhull died January 29, 2013, at the age of 94, and her cremated remains are with her husband's remains at Arlington.

I thought I would be relieved when the research was completed for the last soldier, James Woodhull. He achieved a great deal in life, particularly his humanitarian accomplishments after returning from war. But finishing the last sentence on Woodhull's short biography meant saying goodbye to the men of Company D. In that moment, I had a feeling of loss. I was disappointed because I had been able to contact so few individuals directly connected with the men who signed the flag. And as far as I could determine, none of the men from D Company was alive to talk with me.

However, I had answered many of the questions posed at the beginning of my research. I wanted to know where these citizen soldiers came from. I found they came from all over, from the East Coast to the West, Atlantic to Pacific, from sixteen states. From great cities and towns and also from the most rural hamlets throughout our country. Their backgrounds were as varied as the population makeup of the states from which they came.

Those from rural areas had tended to drop out of school to work on the farm during their high school years. The remainder were usually high school graduates. Alfred Langberg's obituary listed him as a pre-war graduate of Drexel University. Leo Bloom was identified as a student from Baltimore City College when he went into service. And James Woodhull was a 1937 graduate of the University of Vermont. As noted earlier, he later earned a Ph.D. at Pennsylvania State University.

Most of the men were born in the years 1920 to 1924 and most were between 20 and 21 years old. The last D Company soldier to die on the list was Paul Allen in 2016. Most of the men were laid to rest in their local cemeteries among their relatives. Records show five were buried in national military cemeteries. Wilfred Campbell is buried at Fort Logan National Cemetery in Denver. Newton Corbitt is buried at the National Cemetery in Nashville. Ray Johnson is buried at Tahoma National Cemetery in Kent, Washington. Lester Simon's grave is at Jefferson Barracks National Cemetery in St. Louis. And James Woodhull's remains are at Arlington National Cemetery.

After this examination of Bud Blanton's life, I now count myself among the individuals who remember the Timberwolves. It is an honor to be linked to them, even if only through research and an occasional personal family contact. The research has given me a deeper appreciation of sacrifice, of duty to country and devotion to ideals that are greater than any single one of us. Not only my uncle, but all the men who signed the flag have become a part of me. I know them as one might recall dear acquaintances from a long time past. And I hold out the hope that through this book and the people who will read it, I might have the opportunity to meet more family members of the men who signed the flag. Would that not be an inspiring way to continue this journey?

Epilogue

Rest Easy, Men

I began with a simple goal: to write about one man's life and to give a relatively brief typed copy of that story to a 96-year-old aunt I dearly love. But the effort slowly expanded into a complex look at my family and the lives of dozens of men and women I came to know in the months after that bag of letters and photos literally tumbled into my lap.

We have a tradition in our family begun by my cousin Cindy LeGette, daughter of Betty Blanton Mincey and her husband, World War II sailor C. P. Mincey. On the occasion of family birthdays, the individual being honored is asked to give words of wisdom to those attending. You are expected to offer your thoughts on what has been important in shaping your life. The last time I spoke at length, I said I wished every person could experience the sense of pride I felt when I wore the uniform of my country half a century before. I know from his letters that my uncle had that same sense of pride. He never complained, except for wanting more mail. He fit in with the soldiers of Company D on the front line. At his core, he was an Horry County farmer's son, confident he could outwalk and outwork the men with whom he served. He was diligent in learning the tasks of an infantryman, which meant preparing for combat. Simply put, he was a good soldier.

In the summer of 1970, I stood on Alexanderplatz in East Berlin in a US Army uniform. I was there as a private first class carrying out in a minor way the mission to enforce the right of access provisions of the World War II agreement on Berlin, still a divided city a quarter century after peace in Europe.[1] Soldiers like me were dropped off in the East and encouraged to walk around, enjoy a meal, go shopping, literally show the US flag in the Soviet Zone. Alexanderplatz, a place of devastation in May

1945, has been transformed by the Communist regime into the showcase of East Berlin. The expansive square, flanked by modern shops, restaurants, and a fine hotel, attracted thousands of visitors daily.[2]

On that day in East Berlin, I walked miles, shopped for books, and finally ordered the most expensive meal in the best restaurant I could find. And I thought about my uncle. About how he never made it to the end. He never saw Berlin, the capital of his defeated enemy. Or even caught a glimpse of the Russian forces streaming west. More important, he never returned home to see his mother and sisters and brothers and his girlfriend Dot.

It took another nineteen years for Bud Blanton's war to truly end when, in November 1989, the Berlin Wall came down. I was there as a reporter and recognized this remarkable event as something my uncle should have witnessed. Perhaps some of his old Company D buddies who survived the war had watched the fall of the Wall on TV and recognized it as the final chapter in their war. The day the Wall opened I cracked a piece of it loose with a borrowed sledgehammer and two days later mailed the half-pound chunk to Nichols. Had Bud Blanton lived he would have been among the first to touch that piece of history. Today, that Wall souvenir is a gritty, rusting reminder of my long connection to Germany. It sits in a glass container atop the bookcase that now holds Bud Blanton's lost letters.[3]

My brief exploration of the lives of the Timberwolf soldiers who signed the captured Nazi flag makes it clear there was scant recognition in life or death for what they and the millions of other service members accomplished in World War II. Looking at their lives from the distance of three generations, it seems only a precious few got the credit they deserved. There were parades for some upon their return, but memory quickly faded about their achievements. Few of the men ever again discussed at length what had happened to them in the war. The business of getting on with their lives and rebuilding their country took precedence.

There was usually only a brief mention of World War II service in the obituaries of the men I have written about. In particular, I think about Lester F. Simon of Glencoe, Missouri, a wounded recipient of the Silver Star. I could find for him only a forty-word obituary devoid of any mention of his service. I think also of the young, local men whose final sacrifice I never knew about until Bud Blanton's letters pointed me to them and their resting places in our local cemetery. That group included Vincent Astor Ford, the Marine lieutenant awarded the Silver Star for valor in combat on Guam.

It was ironic and touching that Paul Allen, one of the signers of the captured flag and a decorated D-Company hero, lamented late in his life that there had been no parades at all for the men and women he witnessed coming home from Vietnam. And I wish I had met William R. Lawless Sr., of West Pelzer, South Carolina, to thank him for his service and to console him and his wife Doris for the loss of their son in Vietnam more than twenty years after the end of World War II. In addition, I have deep regret for not knowing about the lives of Marshall and Orilla Watts who lived on my street in Nichols. I could have thanked them had I known two of their sons in uniform never lived to see home again.

Bud Blanton saw Europe at its worst and vowed in his letters never to go back once he made it home. Unlike my uncle, I saw Europe in depth, the good and the bad, from the British Isles to the Russian border, and willingly spent four decades of my adult life there. By the time of my first arrival in 1969, the Jerrys (as Bud Blanton called the enemy) had become the industrious Germans of the *Bundesrepublik Deutschland,* an ally and linchpin for the North Atlantic Treaty Organization in the Cold War.

Because of my research I now visit two places with a distinctly different impression than before discovery of the letters. First is Riverside Cemetery across the Lumber River from Nichols. In years past, I normally visited on special days, primarily to touch the gravestone of my cousin, US Army Sergeant Ben M. Brown Jr. Ben was the son of my father's sister Annell Walker Brown, and the husband of Sue Page Brown. He was a hero who did make it home but died much too early, leaving us to grieve his loss. Since reading my uncle's letters, I know Riverside to be a place of many heroes in addition to Ben.

A *Stars and Stripes* colleague, former editor Brian Brooks, observed: "I suspect there are many other families across the country that have such marvelous collections of photos and war letters and don't know what to do with them. All of those stories should be told."[4] He is right and time is dwindling for family members to collect the material and tell those stories, particularly for World War II. Whether it be a book, a photo album, or a simple typewritten account complete with letters and other war memorabilia, the effort should be made to preserve a family's record of its service to country.

I sat with a US soldier on a hill in Kosovo, deep in the Balkan region of the former Yugoslavia. We were looking down at the rolling expanse where US troops would soon build a base to assist in keeping the fragile peace after the NATO bombing campaign against Serbia in 1999. The ceasefire there was tenuous. A day before, a farmer had been shot to death plowing his field as the sporadic fighting between the ethnic Albanian Kosovars and the Serbian militia continued. I looked into the face of this soldier who told me he came from rural Kansas. He was fuzzy-cheeked and happy and open and yet fierce-looking with his rifle and his combat gear. I could swear I saw my uncle's bright eyes in his face and I wondered if the soldier, certainly not yet 20 years old, and perhaps the youngest private in his company like Bud Blanton, would be talking that night to someone back home about what it was like to be far from family in a distant and danger-ous place. I did not ask him any reporter questions. I just enjoyed being in his presence. I told him with pride that the packaged ready to eat meals we were eating were prepared in South Carolina at Mullins where I went to high school.[5] He nodded and told me about wheat fields and the two sisters and parents he left behind when he deployed.

I never met my uncle, but I am certain he was like that young soldier, and it was clear to me we all shared a bond. It linked the two of us there and Bud Blanton and the other soldiers of D Company I have written about. That bond starts the moment you don the uniform of our country and wear the US flag on your arm for the first time. And it does not end when you take the uniform off for the last time. It never ends.

When you are young, you rarely see the way forward clearly. There is no master plan. You make momentous decisions without knowing the path upon which you will be launched. You seek to find your way and with luck things turn out well. However, fate decided the key events in Bud Blanton's life. His father died and he had to become the man of the family. His country called and he had to go. He joined willingly with other brave men and women in a fight to preserve freedom. And he died in that noble effort.

His letters have helped me understand that when the shadows get longer and the years dwindle to a few, there is great comfort in knowing yourself and your family and what went into making you the person you have become. With that knowledge, I can comfortably say farewell one last time to Fletcher "Bud" Blanton. To him and to all the Timberwolves I say: Rest easy, men. There will always be a light on here in Nichols for you and for all the families everywhere in the United States of America who treasure your memory.

ACKNOWLEDGMENTS

Thanks first to my grandmother, Jessie Mae Graham Blanton; my mother, Clarise Blanton Walker; and my father, William S. Walker, for saving Bud Blanton's letters. For the two women it must have involved a great deal of pain. The letters were the last memories of the Blanton family's fallen eldest son. They recognized that his letters, most of them never seen by his siblings, needed to be preserved.

Once I decided to write about the letters, the most important person in the project was my aunt, Betty Blanton Mincey. She was my only direct link with my uncle from his childhood until his death in January 1945. We made a great team, a 70-something reporter and his 96-year-old sidekick seeking to unravel a 77-year-old story of considerable complexity.

Betty and C. P. Mincey's eldest son, Charles Fletcher Mincey, provided superb research support for this project. Simply put, this book could not have been completed without the help of Charles Mincey and the able support of his wife Frankie.

In researching this book, I came to know Betty Floyd Ray, the last remaining sibling of Bud Blanton's best friend Hayden Floyd. Hayden, like Bud, was killed in World War II. And Betty Ray has done her part to keep the memory of her fallen brother alive.

Brittie Blanton Strickland had been a good friend of another fallen soldier, Gary Frank Blanton. At 93 she still retained a sharpness of memory that helped build a written record of my uncle's best friend. And Gary's nephew Frankie Blanton provided full documentary information on his uncle's service to country.

Bud Blanton's wartime friend and fellow soldier Willie Bishop was lucky to have two individuals who continue to cherish his memory—Kim Patterson of Easley, South Carolina, his daughter by marriage, and Wendy

Batey, of Greer, South Carolina. Wendy is Willie Bishop's daughter with Dolly Watson.

Thanks to Kellie Sue Wallace of Clayton, Georgia. Her grandfather, Cecil Atkins, brought home the captured Nazi flag with the signatures of many of the young men who served with Bud Blanton in Company D. Her notes on some of the soldiers who signed the flag provided valuable assistance in tracking their lives after the war.

None of the four book projects I have completed since returning to the US from Europe could have been published without my friend Sammy Watts. Sammy keeps me on the road for research trips with superb maintenance of my vehicles and, in addition to that, he has generously shared the wisdom of his experience about family, the military, work, and living life on an even keel in an increasingly complex world.

My friend Ronald Collins, a high school classmate and Vietnam combat veteran, supported my work by assuming many of the tasks at my farm on days when I had to write. Without his support it would have taken far longer to write this book.

Rosanne Black, director of the Marion County Museum, has provided support for all my writing projects over the past 10 years. Thanks to her for all she does to support writers and artists in the Pee Dee region.

My cousin, Dr. L. L. Gaddy, a successful author in his own right, suggested the University of South Carolina (USC) Press for this book project. At USC Dr. Ehren Foley, the acquisitions editor at USC Press, provided invaluable support in suggesting ways to improve the manuscript. Thanks to the outstanding USC Press team that has worked on this project. I was privileged to work with the Editorial, Design, and Production (EDP) team: Ana Bichanich, Director of EDP; Ashley Mathias, Digital Publishing Coordinator; Kerri Tolan, Production Editor; and Ida Audeh, Copyeditor. Additional thanks go to Cathy Esposito, Marketing and Sales Director; and Dianne Wade, Marketing Assistant, who showed immediate interest and came up with many good suggestions to introduce the book to readers. Thanks also to Mary Ann Lieser, the book indexer. Additionally, noted writing coach Kelly Boyer Sagert first pointed out the potential of this book project and offered valuable assistance and advice as leader of a seminar on memoir writing.

Special thanks to my first writing coach and life mentor, the late Dr. L. L. Henry of Clemson, South Carolina. Thanks also to the late Dr. Daniel Walker Hollis whose teaching at USC led me to international studies and an eventual history doctorate at a German university. And thanks also to Dr. Jerry Reel at Clemson University for his lively and inspiring history instruction. Additional thanks during my doctoral studies to Drs. Heinz-Dietrich Löwe, Svetlana Ressel and Edgar Wolfrum at Ruprecht-Karls-Universität in Heidelberg, Germany.

My special thanks to my friends the Adams—Klaus, Martha, and Sabine, plus Mike—in Wolfskehlen, Germany. They provided feedback and support during the research and writing of the book. Also in Germany, thanks to Peter Batty's daughters Monika and Evelyn for accepting our family immediately when we first came to meet them. And to *Stars and Stripes* colleagues Peter Jaeger (Heidi), Bern Zovistoski, Kevin Dougherty, Mike Abrams and the late Bob Wicker and his widow Kathy.

My lifetime friend, attorney Charles Hill of Jackson, South Carolina, and Columbia, South Carolina, read the unfinished manuscript, made writing suggestions, and served as a sounding board for improving the book. Thanks to him and his wife Frances, as always, for support and writing advice. Thanks also to lifetime friends Dan and Judy Speights, (Hampton), Terry and Gail Richardson (Barnwell), Barney and Lou Easterling (Kingstree), Don and Susan Shelley (Greenville), William and Barbara Holton (Nashville, Tennessee), David and Jan Redden (Seneca) and Paul Burnette (Pendleton) for their intellectual stimulation and encouragement of my writing projects. For their support of my writing over the years, I thank Sue Page Brown, Susan Gehring, Tina Cirillo, Everett McMillian, James McNeill, Ruben Thompson, James Scott, Ken Hanke, the late Frank Smith, Mary Alice Thompson, Wise Batten, Jimmy Burton, Billy Ware, Keith Waters, Dave Christopher, Gordon Edgin, Chris Clancy, Charlie Compton, John Dickerson, Al Crosby, Jim Hill, Ted Petoskey, Al Roach, Don Sharp, Bill Speights, Hank Theiling, Buddy Thompson, Johnny Parker, Ronnie Wingard, Jim Prather, Flip Phillips, the late Carlyle Henley and his widow Mott, Larry Young, Phil and Debbie Cunningham, Tony and Cyndi Biggs, Johnny McCumber, Candace Everett, Gene and Deb Knudsen, James Scott, Janet Nord, LaFon and Cindy LeGette, Van and Adrienne Jones, Bo McMillan, Karen Edwards, Kathy Jo Gaddy, Jerry Bane, Judy Davis and her late husband Jim, Charlie and Frances Bethea, Johnny Ray Floyd, Jimmy and Sara Anne Devers, Bud and Martha Ellerbe, John and Vicki Kirby, Sam and Jill McMillan, Ella Moore, Harriet Enzor, Butch and Jeanette Pace, Jim and Catherine Battle, Katherine McCormick and her late husband Malcolm, Jim Huggins, Jean Berry, Billy Daniel, Dr. Lacy Edmison, Dr. Lyndsi Cress, Mike and Mary Beth Simmons, Brian and Anne Brooks, Frank and Margy Roehl, Dale and Karol Peyton, Norm and Sally Cotter, Dan and Joyce Basarich, Tom Posey and his late wife Freida, Ricardo and Maria Elena Sanchez, Bill and Heidrun Erwin, Mark and Kirsten Garcia, Norm and Libby Zeigler, Euel and Mary Ann Shelley, Albert and Irma Finocchiaro, Zoran, Amira, Andrea and Anya Petkovic, Dragan Petkovic, Adel Ismail, Thomas and Rada Zeh, Larry and Janice Walker, Jay and Barbara Walker, Archie and Twila Bates, Gary and Cheryl McClellan, Will and Debbie Johnson, Cody and Megan Herring, Marcia Mincey, Joe and Cindy Gibbs, Kent Williams, Lucas Atkinson, Randy Bryant, Bev Filer, Patty Brown, Sandra Brown Turbeville, Sonny and Sylvia Tanner, Tom and Judy Luke, Roger and Linda Yorde, Dr. Kenneth Mincey and Lisa Mincey, Lee Grant, Maurice and Milton Page, P. L. Elvington, Janice Wood, Ben Sclair, James Scott, Beth Pond, the late Dr. Joan Wilcox, Tom and Rosi Hlavacek, Barbara Ferg Carter, and Dolly Alvarez.

Finally, thanks to my wife, Elizabeth McRae Walker. She has been my best friend and closest advisor on writing projects through fifty-five years of marriage and counting. Without her support this book, and the others before it, would never have been possible.

APPENDIX A

The Letters

All letters have been transcribed as written with no grammar or spelling changes.

July 2, 1944
at camp

Dearest mama

I bet you are cooking Dinner while I am writing this letter. I would like to be at home to eat dinner today. It sure is lonesome up here on Sunday. I hate to see Sunday come. When I am working I don't think much about going home but when Sunday comes I sure want to go home. I wonder if you are getting all of my mail. I don't think you are because I haven't heard from you but one time this week. I heard from Dot 3 times Friday. All of the letters were mailed different days. An I heard from her 2 Saturday. I hope I get a lot of mail today. I wrote you and asked about (Aunt) Florence's address. I might go to see her some weekend. There is a boy up here that has a girl in Savannah. An I can go with him. All of the boys in my hut got a weekend pass this weekend but about three of us. You could send me James Colon Grainger address. I might go to see him some time. Write me often and tell Edna and Clarise an all of the family to write me.

Lots of love
Bud

Postcard dated July 16, 1944, showing a Royal Ponciana Tree, Florida

From Bud Blanton to Mrs. F. S. Blanton
Today I had the chance to go home this weekend but the trip cost to much. The boy wanted $20 bucks. I wouldn't give over $10 bucks if I had it. I sure

would like to go home but I will have to stand it out here a while longer. Write soon.

Love Bud

Postcard dated July 28, 1944, with a picture of a beauty spot in Florida

From Bud Blanton to Mrs. F. S. Blanton

Hello mama

Wonder what you are doing this hot afternoon. We have been working long hours this week. I haven't had my shoes off in 2 days. I worked all day and had to stand guard duty last night. I sleep at the guard house and could not pull off my shoes. I have a night problem until 1230.

Love Bud

Tuesday night

Dearest Mama

I don't have much time to write. Its almost time for the lights to go out. I wont get time to write tomorrow or Thursday. We are going to camp out tomorrow night. Write me when you can. I get my mail when I can out in the field. I heard from Sal an Edna today. I hope I hear from you tomorrow. I washed a few clothes for some boys tonight. They pay plenty an I am going to need the money anyway an I dont mind washing them. Write soon an be good

Love Bud

Summer 1944 basic training

I received the candy an shaving cream Wed.

Love Bud

Thursday morning

Dearest Mama,

Here I am again writing you before day. Its not but a few minutes before we start to work. I got a letter from Bessie an Dot Wed. I hear from dot almost ever day. I wrote Will but I haven't heard from him yet. We had quite a bit of trouble here in Camp Blanding last night. The ammunition storage caught on fire. I dont think it did much harm just scared ever body good.

Its not but . . . weeks training that we have now it wont be long before we will go home.

I started writing this letter before we went to work this morning but didn't finish it. I happened to have a Lt pick me an 2 more boys to help him load dumb rounds in a machine gun today as we didn't have to go out with our co. It was the easiest work I have done since I have been in the army.

Our Co. commander received orders last night that we were not to have any more speed marches or cary any more heavy packs. The captain told us last night that this week would be the hardest week we would have an that so far but it Thursday night an it easier than any week we have had since we have been here so far. I got back to camp before the rest of the company. an one of the Sargents just came in an said that one of the boys got shot in the shoulder.

The Captain told us today that we were to get up at 5 o clock tomorrow morning an go out in the woods an practice close combat until 2 oclock Saturday morning before day. He said that would be the hardest day in our cicle. I wont have time to write you tomorrow but I will write you Sat. night. I guess I had better close an write Dot an clean my rifle. Tell Betty if she doesn't write me I am not going to kiss her. Tell all of the family to write me. I want all of you to be sure to write the next two weeks for I will be camping out.

Love Bud

Postcard August 1, 1944, with picture of a beauty spot in Florida

From Bud Blanton to Mrs. F. S. Blanton
Wonder what you are doing this morning. Received a letter from Betty one day. I will get Son something for his birthday when I get time. Tell ever body to write. I havent got much mail till last week. (Last sentence is not legible)

Postcard August 4, 1944, with ph oto of water hyacinths in Florida

From Bud Blanton to Mrs. F. S. Blanton
Dearest mama
Wonder what you are doing today. I have been to the dentist today and have had 4 teeth pulled. Didnt hurt much and my mouth feels better now. Got a

cake from Edna today. Sure was good to get it. Anything from home is better than anything I buy. Write soon and be good.

Love Bud

Tuesday morning
August 22, 1944

Dearest mama,

How are you this early in the morning. Its 5 o'clock. Now we get up at a quarter till four and eat breakfast an made up my bed an sweep the floor and now I am writing you. Now we will have to start to work in a few minutes. I didn't hear from you yesterday. Hope I hear from you today. If I don't have time to finish this letter before I go to work I will finish it at dinner. We have to stay out in the wood Wed. night. We had the hottest weather yesterday that we had had since I have been up here. I guess you have already hear the war news when you get this letter. But the American flag was up in paris last night. Wont be long before the war is over.

Love Bud
P.S.
Write soon and tell Betty to write

Mid-September 1944 basic training

Sunday evening

Dearest mama

Just received a letter from you. It was mailed Saturday for it was wrote Friday night. I was very glad to hear from you yesterday and I was feeling blue last night an this morning. I heard from Dot today an this letter she wrote was mailed the 14th of September and the one you wrote was mailed the 16th and I got them both at the same time. I don't see why I got these letters at the same time. I wrote Sal this morning and I wrote C. P. today. You said you couldn't get a bag for me at Mullins. You could write Vera and have her to get me one. I no she could get one for a soldier . . . like that. She could buy it and send it on to me. You asked me if I had any money. I don't have but a $1 or $2 but it doesn't matter. I get along on that until time to go home. I sure hate to ask you for the money to buy my ticket to the next camp but I will have to. It will be quite a lot if I go to Ft. Mead. It will cost about $30.00. If I go to California it will cost about $45.00 but I will get it back when I get to the next camp. An I can give it back to you then. This doesn't sound very convincing but I will be sure to get the money back. I wonder how Hubert Strickland is getting along with the car. He sure got a worn out car when he got it. I sure am glad you sold it being you got that much money out of it. I don't have any way to go any place when I go home. How did you go to Mullins. Who did you get to take you? I bet Son an Ralph are tickled about their new clothes. I remember proud I was of my Brown suit when you bought it. It was something to be proud of. All of my clothes I have got in the Army are new. Some of the boys got clothes that had been worn before. I sure . . . nice field jacket if they let me keep it. They may take it. our summer clothes before we leave here. But we get another coat before we leave I think.

C. P. said that some of the boys where he was couldn't stand to march very much. There is a lot of boys here that can do hard march than I can but there is nobody here that can march any farther than I can. I never been so tired since I been here that I couldn't march 2 miles more. I haven't had a blister on my feet since I have been in the Army. Some of the boys had blisters on their feet. An they had to keep marching on the blisters on their feet. An the blisters on their feet burst and make sores. Now they have sores on their feet and have to make the 25 mile hike like that. Some of the boys ankles are swelled and have been swelled since the 8 or 9 week. My ankles swelled up until you couldn't tell I had any ankles the 8 or 9 weeks But they didn't stay swelled long. I wouldn't tell you about it then but I afraid you might think I was working too hard but working doesn't hurt my body. I can prove that by you.

I guess Betty is proud of the watch C. P. gave her. I no I would be. I think I will try to go to town this last weekend I am here. I only have 3 more weeks. I will be glad when tomorrow comes for it time to start back to work and the more days I work the less time we have to stay . . . (indistinguishable). Who is Willadine dating?

Tell everybody hello and write soon
Love Bud

Friday morning
Sept. 16, 1944

Dearest mom

How are you this morning. Hope you are feeling fine and enjoying life. I am feeling fine only I would like to have something else to eat. We get good meals and bread but you don't get near enough for the work you do. The co. commander said that there was no packages to be brought out but the mailman is bringing out packages ever day. So I want you to send me one as quick as you get this letter. You will get this letter Sunday I guess an you can send the package Monday an I will get it Tuesday. I want you to send me some candy an good crackers and a cake an a few bags of salted peanuts. I guess you think I cost you a lot lately. The next thing I send after will be money to go home an can buy my ticket to my next camp. I heard from Vera yesterday and Sal and you. I sure like to get mail because it's sure lonesome out here. We worked part of the night last night an have two hours off this morning. I haven't had much time to write for we have been busy. We had to dig trenches to stay in Thursday night because there was a Hurricane coming this way.

I dreamed last night that Son was dead and I went home to his funeral on a motorcicle. Tell ever body Hello and tell the family to write.

Love Bud

Sept. 25, 1944, postcard with a cartoon cow on it

From Bud Blanton to Mrs. F. S. Blanton [The pencilled message is fading and some the postcard cannot be read.]
How are you this afternoon. It is 11 o'clock at night and I have just got back from the show. I heard from you and sal and clarise today. I will write you a letter soon.
Lots of Love Bud

United States Army

Oct 1, 1944

Dearest mama

I wonder what you could be doing this morning. I am not working for a change. I have just eaten breakfast. I am going to clean up and go to see

Elbert Clark. I didn't hear from you or Dot yesterday. I sure hope I hear from you today. I will close an I will write again. Write soon.

Undated postcard from Baltimore

Dearest Vera,

I wonder what you are doing tonight. I have been writing Mama an Dot. I haven't had very much time to write while I have been here. I will write you a long letter when I get to my next camp. I am leaving in the morning. I guess I will be in France in a week an a half. I enjoyed staying that day with you very much. I have to close now. Bye Love Bud

Vmail

Nov. 4, 1944

Dearest mama

I am wondering what you are doing while I am writing this letter. I guess you have already heard from me a few times. I have been getting more to eat than I . . . have before. We are having lots of rain but it is not to cold. I dont write very often for I dont ever stay one place long enough. I havent heard from any of you yet. It wont be very long before I get some mail I hope.

Mama, I wonder if the war is about to end. It would be fine if it would end this minute. I didnt realize what was happening over here until I saw for myself. The two boys I am telling you about are not with me now. They are not left together rather all three of us . . . I think the germans will surrender before long. There is no need for them to fight on for they are already beaten. I will write ever chance I get. So keep sweet and write often. I hope you have a fine Christmas.

Lots of Love Bud

November 23, 1944
In France

Dearest Mama

I wonder what you are doing today. I am fine. I just hope all of you are as well as I am. I have just eaten a big Thanksgiving dinner. I eat all the turkey I could hold. We are getting better to eat than we have ever had before we came across. I hope I get some mail soon. I will write ever chance I get. And that wont be very often. I want you to have all of the family to write me. I want Will an C. P. to write me to. I wont get to give any of you anything for Christmas. Please buy Son and Ralph something and tell them I sent it to them.

Dont forget to get Dot a nice present. I hope Will can get a set of pencils like the ones he gave Clarise. If he cant you can get a nice dinner set. I wont write an ask for a Christmas present for it will be too much trouble for you to send it. But if there is any way you can send me 3 or 4 pairs of wool boot socks number 9. I am in Normandy France. Mama tell ever body hello an to write. I will write again when I can. I am going to write Dot now.

Forever your son
Bud

Nov 26, 1944
In France

Dearest Mama

I wonder what you are doing now. I have just eaten supper. I guess you are getting ready to eat dinner. I am still in France. I was in England at one time. I sure hope I hear from you soon. But I guess it will be a long time before I do hear from home. I wonder how the war is getting along now. I dont ever hear any war news now for I can't read french papers. We cant spend very much money over hear. All we can buy is 2 packs of cigarettes a week an 2 bars of candy. I think you can buy wine an sider in town but I am not ever going to start back drinking so I can save most of the money I get while I am over here for I no I will need some money when I get back home. I am hoping this war will hurry an stop for I no lots of the boys are being killed. I want to stay over here until the war is over for if I ever go back to the states I wouldn't come back. I visited La Havre France not long ago. Mama there is lots of things that I would like to tell you. But it would be cut out by the cinsor. But I am well and in no danger at all an getting better to eat than I did when I was taking my training. Mama if you dont hear from me often you should no that something is wrong with the mail or that I didn't have time to write. If I dont write often I will still be think of you all. Tell everybody to write and be good.

Love

V-Mail

Dec. 5, 1944
In Germany

Dearest Mama

How are you and all the family. I am okay only I am so full. We get more to eat than we can eat. I haven't gotten any mail from anyone yet but I don't think it will be so long before I hear from you. I wrote you yesterday and I also wrote Dot. Today is a cold fair day. It snowed some yesterday. I bet you could guess what I did yesterday. I took a bath that was the first bath I have had since I have been over here. I havent had a hair cut since a week before I left the states. I have been trying to get it cut but no one seems to cut hair. There is no place to spend my money over here. I havent been paid yet. I am going to send this money home when I get paid if there is any way. Tell ever body hello an write me often. I may not write often but dont worry for I want have time to write much. I am the youngest pvt in my company.

Love an Luck Bud

Dec. 7, 1944
In Germany

Dearest Mama

I wonder how you an all of the family are tonight. I am fine I guess. I haven't heard from home yet. I hope I hear soon. I wonder if C. P. has had a furlough yet. You tell him an Will to stay in the states if there is any chance. I am about to realize what the war is all about.

I wish part of the men back home could see how it is over here. I bet they would go an get under the bed at home an stay there until after the war is over instead of going out and having a different movie ever night. I often think about how lucky some of the people back home are an about how foolish I used to do when I was back home. I used to go out with some girl and spend all of the money you had or most of it. That was about a year ago. An about 3 or 4 times a week I would get high. I never did get enough sleep. Instead of doing that now I go to bed when I get a chance an pray that this war will be over soon instead of thinking about where I would go the next night. This is a crazy time to think about something like that but it is all true. Mom I wont get very much money a month but I am going to send it home so I will have a little when I get back. When they get candy and stuff like that over here it doesnt cost you anything. It is divided among the company.

Three years ago this war was declared. I dont think this thing can go much longer. I can't understand why the Germans keep on fighting since they are beaten so bad. President Roosevelt could stop this war today if he wanted to. I think an about all of the boys over here thinks the same. I sent out a few Christmas cards. They were sorry cards but they were the best I had.

Some of the boys heard from home an their mothers had a message that they were wounded in action. But they were as well as ever. So if you ever hear that I am wounded or anything is wrong think nothing of it for they get things mixed up over hear. I hope I never get in battle but if I do I will trust in the Lord and do my best.

Tell Son and Ralph to be good an I will be home before long. I will write them a letter when I get time. I will write ever time I can so goodbye for this time an be good.

Lots of Love an Luck
Bud

In Germany
Dec. 8

Dearest Mama,

I wonder what you and the rest of the family are doing tonight. I guess you all joined around the fire talking an they are studying. I bet Son and Ralph are telling about something that Delano Stroud said or done. I remember when they used to tell about something that happened at school that day. That was back in the good old days. Mama I guess you havent heard from me very often for I havent had time to write very much. I wonder if you received the money order that I sent home. I am going to send a little home ever month. If it is not more than $10.00 or $15.00 it will help a little. If I was to send $15.00 a month and the $10.00 bond I have out that would be $25.00 ever month. And if this war lasts as long as I think it will I will have a good little sum of money. And I sure will need it after I get home. I want to run a store after the war. I never dont want a lot of money. I just want enough for me and you Son and Ralph to live good on. For I no Betty and Bessie will be married when I get back.

Mama, you don't get very blue over here. In fact I dont think about home as much as you do when you are in the states. There is always something else to think of. I sure would like to get some mail. I dont believe the mailman knows where I stay at now.

I will write as often as I can an I want you to do the same. Tell all of the family to write me and I will answer them if I get time.

Tell Son and Ralph to be good boys and I will be home as soon as I help run down the rest of the jerries. An I hope that wont be long.

Mama send me a book of air mail stamps for they are hard to get up here. Be good and write.

Lots of Love and Luck

Bud

P.S. Please excuse this German stationary. It's all I have so it will have to do.

Somewhere in Germany

Dec. 10, 1944

Dearest Mama

I wonder what you are doing tonight. I guess you are all getting along fine. I am fine. I have been a little blue today. I sent . . . (not readable) a Christmas card and wrote a letter on the back of it. I guess she will be surprised to hear from me.

I still haven't heard from . . . (not readable) I sure hope I hear back from youall before Christmas. I have been writing you ever day almost. I have been writing Dot to. I sent Edna Clarise and Vera a Christmas card. It may be after Christmas before they get them. I was looking at my pictures today an found . . . (not readable) address on the back of the pictures

Some of the older men in this Co said that we were not very far from . . . not readable) company.

Mama I write ever time I can. I will still write when I can. Tell ever body hello. An please write me.

Lots of Love an Luck

Bud

Somewhere in Germany

Dec 12, 1944

Dearest Mama

How are you all tonight. I am fine I guess. I am still getting plenty to eat an not working very hard. I am cooking a rabbit now. I wish you were here to help me eat it. We are staying in houses now. They are lots of apple orchards here an the houses has lots of apples in them. An they sure are good. I wish I had a ham or a part of one. I think some pork would be good now. You can send me a package after Christmas if you can. I hope I hear from you soon. I write ever time I can so please write often and be good.

Lots of Love

BUD

Dec 13, 1944

Dearest Mama,

How are you today. I am fine. I haven't heard from home yet. I hope I hear soon. I have written almost ever day. I hope I have time from now on to write ever day but I no I wont. I guess I will get lots of mail when it does catch up with me.

The time sure does past fast here. I have been left the states over a month. The ship that I came to France on was sunk about 15 minutes after I got off. See I was lucky that I didn't sink to. You cant say anything more when you are writing it always has to be. I dont like the way it sounds but it is still the cencors order.

Mama I have just gotten a haircut and I sure feel lots cleaner. It was the first one I have had since a week before I left the states.

I wonder if the boys have ever gotten fat. I wish I could be there and help you eat them. I wouldn't be much help in butchering them. I wonder if it is very cold at home now. It is not cold here but it rains here a lot. There is some boys in my company from South Carolina I don't believe the boys that are training now will ever have to come here unless they come to help clean up after the war. Anyway I hope they never have to come across. There are some pretty horses over here but most of them are bob tail. I dont under-stand why they cut their tail off. They dont have anything to fan the flies off of them with their.

This is something to be writing about in a letter but I didn't want to write such a short letter.

I dreamed about Mildred Dorsey last night. I thought I saw her at Mullins an I was setting in the car talking to her. I wish I was at Mullins talking to her now. Tell Betty and Bessie if they see Mildred any time to get her address for me. I would like to write her. I think she would answer my letters. I always like her fine as a friend.

If you dont mind excuse this writing. For I cant lay the blame on the paper. I guess I had better close and write Dot.

I sent Winnie Ford a Christmas card. I wrote an told her on the back of the card that I bet she wouldn't look at it. I guess you remember when I broke a date with her. Well she told me that if I ever broke a date with her that she wouldn't ever date me again. But if I ever get back in the states she is the first girl I am going to date if she will date me. I told her then that I was sorry but I dont guess she will believe it. But I can truthfully say that I hated that after I did it worse than any way I have ever treated a girl. She is the nices girl I have ever dated not excepting none. It would be my luck for her to be married when I get back to the states. Write soon and keep sweet.

Lots of Love and Luck

Bud

Somewhere in Germany

Dec. 14, 1944

Dearest Clarise

How are you doing today. I am fine I guess. I am the fattest I have been since I left the states. I had all the pork chops I could eat at dinner an I have been eating German jelly since I eat dinner. We sure get all we can eat here. I wish you had part of this jelly. I might not eat enough to make me sick. Doesn't this make you hungry. You no I feel sorry for you people back in the states when I get to eating all the rations. I wonder if youall are getting plenty to eat. You will have to excuse this silly letter. I am in a crazy mood today.

Its a little colder here than it has been since I have been here. The ground was froze this morning. Just think its only 11 more days until Christmas. I wish I was home. I sure would like to see Santa Clause. I wonder if there is a Santa Clause in Germany. I bet Santa come over here to get his apples for Christmas. There is so many apples over here. If you see Santa tell him if he has anything for me save it until next Christmas an I might get it then for I will be their. I have some beechnut chewing gum now an I had some mounds candy bars one day this week. I havent been paid since I came across. The government must think I am working for nothing. I couldn't spend my money if I had it so I am satisfied if they dont pay me until I get back to the states I guess. I had better sign off for this time. So keep sweet and write me often.

Lots of Love an Luck

Bud

Somewhere in Germany

Dec. 15, 1944

Dearest Folks

How are you doing now? Guess you are as fine as ever. I still haven't heard from home. I am still hoping to get a letter any day. I expect you have been hearing from me often for I have been writing you ever chance I get. I guess it will be after Christmas when you get this letter. So I hope you had a nice Christmas.

I want you to send me a box an I want you to put a State paper in it. One boy got a box last night an shared it with part of us. He had a fruit cake and I got some of it. It sure was good.

I wonder if you are getting a $10 bond from me. I had one took out of my pay for this coming month. I have just gotten paid. I don't get much but I am going to send what I can of it home. I want to save enough to start a little business of my own when I get out of the Army. I was reading in a paper about some outstanding man not getting enough cigarettes. When the boys over here can't get cigarettes they never say much about it. They are to proud to be living to worry about a little thing like a cigarette. I think he should be ashamed of his self. If I could see him I think I would tell him so.

I wrote Clarise last night. I hope she gets an I hope Son got all of my mail to. I expect to hear soon from one of the boys that come across with me got a package but he hasen't gotten any mail. Mom how about sending me that picture of you Aunt Florence, Aunt Beatrice. I dont have one of you an I remember that picture so if you dont mind I would like to have it. I dont have a picture of Edna or Vera. I have a picture of all of the family besides you an them. I want a picture of you all.

I dreamed about Ralph last night an I thought he was rich. An I thought I was home. I was greatly disappointed when I woke up and found I was in Germany. Dont forget to tell Betty an Bessie to write often. Bye and keep sweet.

Lots of Love an Luck

BUD

In Germany

Dec. 16, 1944

Dearest Mom

I am writing you again. I am writing the same old thing as I do ever day. I dont get any mail so I dont no anything to write. I have written Edna a letter today. I wrote Clarise a letter one day this week an I am going to write Vera the first chance I get. I am wondering if you have been hearing from me. I got paid last night and bought a money order today. I am putting it in this letter an I hope it gets to you. I wont get as much next month for the ten dollar bond will come out of the pay next month. Mama I didn't even know how to count my money when I got it. But I soon found it. I am drinking a can of Grapefruit juice. It sure is sour but it gives you a appetite. We had zuccinnis for supper and hamburgers for dinner. A boy just opened a box from home an gave me some english walnuts an they sure were good. When you send me a box be sure an send a good size box. For the boys I am with now have been in the outfit a long time an are getting lots of boxes an are very nice about sharing with me.

Lots of Love and luck

Bud

Dec. 17, 1944

Dearest Mom

Here it is Sunday evening just eight days until Christmas. I just found out it was Sunday a few minutes ago. I keep up with the date but I dont keep up with the days. We haven't had any rain in about a week. I hope it doesn't rain again in a month or two. I guess you think ever time I write I am talking about eating well. One of the boys got three packages today. One of them had a big fruit cake in it. They have lots of fireworks here than they do in the states only they are a different kind of fire works. I dont like to write V mail but its all I have to write on. But I guess it will go home quicker. I am going to write Vera when I get through here. Keep sweet an write often an I hope you all have a nice Christmas. Tell Son and Ralph hello.

Lots of Love

BUD

In Germany

Dec. 18, 1944

Dearest Mama

How are you and all of the family getting along these days. I hope you are all fine. I am getting along fine. I guess you think all I write is about something to eat. Well I am eating mixed nuts now an boy are they good. I haven't gotten any mail yet. I am just waiting and hoping. I have some clean clothes on one more time. I have written ever one in the family now an I am not going to write very much until I hear from home for I dont no anything to write. Write soon an keep sweet.

Lots of Love an Luck

BUD

In Germany

Christmas Night

Dearest Mama

I wonder what you are doing tonight. I am fine I guess. I have had a nice Christmas dinner an some hershey candy. I hope you are all fine. I haven't got any mail yet. I am still hoping to get some soon. I am a messenger now. I sure am glad I was changed. My Sargent is from N.C. an is a good Sargent. Tell everbody Hello an write soon. I haven't written for about five days now but I write ever chance I get. Tell Ralph an Son Hello.

Lots of Love

Bud

In Germany
Dec. 28, 1944
Three Oclock
At Night

Dearest Mama

Here I am writing you again tonight. I have just gotten my mail and I sure was surprised to get some mail. I got 2 letters from you and 2 from Dot. One of your letters were mailed the 13 of Nov and one the 17 of Nov. The ones from Dot were mailed the 13–14 of Nov. You said in the letters that Ralph leg was broken and that you had just brought him out of the hospital. You didn't tell me how he got it broke it or any thing about it. You had already told me about it in another letter but I had never gotten the other letter.

Mama you also told me about Betty and C. P. being married. Well I guess if they were going to get married that one time was as good as another. I guess C. P. is as good or better than most of boys. I sure hope Betty stays with you. Tell Betty I would like to give her a wedding present but I couldn't get her anything not where I am now. An anyway I dont guess she expects one. I hope C. P. can be lucky enough to stay in the states. I don't think he would like it over here. I haven't seen any body that did.

Mama I sure would have hated for you to have seen me after I read the letters from you an Dot. I cried worse than I ever have in my life. I dont no what made me do it. But it sure helped my feelings. I have never felt like I did then it seemed like some body back home was dead or something. I just want the rest of my mail to catch up with me so I can find out something about how Ralph got hurt or what happened to him. I guess Ralph thinks he gets his share of going to the hospital an having broken legs. I no you sure have a lot of hospital bills to pay. But I guess we should be proud there is someone to fix people up when they are hurt.

I got Hayden Floyd address now an I no where he is fighting at. He is in the 3rd Army the 25 division and not far from where I am. But I am not in that army. Tell Betty I didn't cry because of her being married an that I hope her a lot of luck an a big bunch of children. Tell Sal to please wait until I get back to get married for it wont seem as much like home if her an Betty is gone.

I guess Son an Ralph will be almost grown when I get back home. An Salley is already grown. Betty will be grown in a year or two.

You said Betty heard from G.R. I sure hope he didn't go to Blanding to take his basic training. You said he still cut a lot of fool. I think it alright to cut fool when you feel like it but over here we dont cut to much fool.

Mama I pray to God ever night that he will carry me through this war safe and get me back home to you and the rest of the family. I also pray for you and everbody back in the states an for the ones over here. Its strange that I had never thought of God before as I do now. But I have asked for his help an deep down in my heart I no he has answered my prayers. Mama keep sweet until I get back and tell everbody hello. I am going to write Son and Ralph a letter now.

Lots of Love an Luck
BUD

In Germany

Dec. 28, 1944

Dearest Mama

Here I am writing you a few lines to let you know that I am still living an getting along fine. I hope you are all well and getting along as good as ever. I haven't heard from any of you yet. I am hoping to hear soon. I sure hope you have been hearing from me often. But I know you haven't for the last week an a half for I haven't had time to write. I know all of you have plenty of time to write so I am expecting a letter ever day from home after I do get my first mail.

I wonder a lot about what is happening back home now. I wonder if you have gotten a $10.00 war bond from the Government yet for you were supposed to get one for it will be taken out of my pay for the month of Dec.

Mama I am sending some german mark home for souvenir. Before the war this money was worth 10¢ per mark. But it cant be used anymore.

Mama I guess you think I want you to send me a lot but I dont guess your mind. If you can I want you to send the shoulder of a small hog. If you dont have one you can get one from someone. You can cut the leg part off so it wont take to big a box. It wont spoil if it is already taken salt. Maybe I wont be in combat when it gets here. I can cook a little now an we have to cook our own. Bye an keep sweet.

Lots of Love an Luck
Bud

In Germany
Dec. 28, 1944

Save this letter an
all others I write

Dear Boys

I wonder what you are doing tonight. I hope you are getting along fine. I am getting along fine as ever. Ralph I heard about our getting your leg broken. I sure was sorry to hear that. I rather it had been my leg than yours. I want you to be good an not worry mama any for she worrys to much already. So I want you an Ralph to be good to each other an not be to mean.

Boys I would almost give my right arm to see you an the rest of the family tonight. It sure is lonesome over here for there no one I know.

Son I don't no where you have studied about Belgium and Holland in school or not but I wish you could see the two countrys. I visited them both once. They sure are beautiful places. Boys I am going to help kill the rest of the jerrys if I have to run them down so I can hurry an get back home to all of you. Boys get mom to take her picture with you an send it to me. By the way how do you boys like your new brother in law. I hope you like him fine. I think he will do for Betty.

Lots of Love
Bud

Dec 29, 1944
In Germany
Dearest Clarise

Wonder what you could be doing tonight. I hope you are getting along fine. I am well an getting plenty to eat. I have a better appetite than I have ever had before. I am getting heavier ever day. I am not getting fat but I am putting on lots of weight. I received a letter from you an mama today. I received 2 letters from mama yesterday an 2 from Dot. I sure was home sick after I read the letters from home about Ralph being hurt an about Betty being married. I haven't gotten all the mail that mama has written me so I don't know how he got hurt an anything about it. I seemed like some one in the family was dead. I guess Sally will be married by the time I get back in the states. I hope she doesn't. I hope that about A.B. is a false report. I sure hated to hear about it. I also hated to hear about Mr. Cross Grainger being dead. Clarise you said that you hoped that my 20th Birthday was an enjoyable one. Well it sure was. I was not on the front line then an that was something to be thankful for. Every thing has been pretty quite the last few days and I have had time to write quite a few letters. I have written ever one in the family since I have been over here. I sure will be glad when I get the rest of my mail so I will no how Ralph got hurt an all about it.

You said in the letter that you hoped that I got my Christmas packages in time for Christmas. Well it is the 29 Dec now an I haven't gotten them but they will be good when they get here. I am thankful that I have gotten some mail already. I just got an interruption for a few minutes an I am rather nervous now.

You said if there was anything that I wanted not to hesitate to ask for it. I thought—excuse this German paper—You knew that I never fail to ask for what I want. I wrote an told mama to send me part of a shoulder but I guess she can't send but five pounds at a time.

Tell Will to take care of his self an write me an be sure to stay in the states. It gets awful rough over here at times. I would write Will but I don't have his address.

I was glad to hear about Winnie working at Mr. Pace. I know she will make a good clerk for she is real smart.

You said that you were all praying that the Lord would watch over me an take me back home safely. Clarise you all are not the only ones that are praying. I ask the lord ever night to keep me safe an bless all of the folks back home an all the people all over the world. He has watched over me this long an I know he will be with me always. Write soon an be good.

Lots of Love an Luck

Bud

December 31, 1944
In Germany

Dearest Mama

How are you today. I hope you are getting along fine. I am fine. I guess you are expecting a letter from me ever day. Well I dont have time to write ever day but I write ever chance I get. I got a letter from you and Clarise day before yesterday. I didnt get any mail yesterday. Clarise said that she hoped that I got my Christmas packages in time for Christmas. I didn't get the letter from her in time for Christmas. I hope I get the boxes before long not that I dont get plenty to eat but I just want to get them. I am getting anything to eat that I want now but I have to cook it. It is all canned food. All that has to be done is to just warm it good. We get lots of jelly an butter cream an coffee.

I hope Ralph is still getting along good. I hated to hear about A.B. being missing in action. Maybe he will turn up soon. He might have gotten lost off from his company. You said that you had gotten the suit case. You said that you hadn't gotten my pictures back yet. I hope they look better than I do. I dont have much time so I will close an write again soon.

Lots of Love an Luck
BUD

Jan. 2, 1945
In Germany

Dearest Mama,

How are you this cold day anyway I guess you are fine. I hope you are all getting along good. I haven't heard from you in about 3 days. I am hoping to get some mail soon. I dont guess it is as cold there as it is here. It snows almost ever day but we have plenty clothes an don't mind the cold very much. I didn't write you yesterday. I wrote Betty one day. I hope she got it already. Mama I dont have time to write a long letter now. I just wanted to write a few lines to let you no that I was well an getting plenty to eat an a warm place to sleep so you wouldn't worry an imagine I was sleeping in a fox hole. Tell everbody hello an to be good. Write when you can.

Lots of Love an Luck
BUD

Jan 3, 1945
In Germany

Dearest Vera

How are you an John E. getting along these cold winter days. I am fine. I guess I have plenty to eat an a warm place to sleep although I am in combat. I have gotten 2 letters from mama 2 from Dot an 1 from Clarise. That sure isn't much mail. I thought that the rest would follow that but it seems to have quit coming. Vera before I left home from my furlough Mama gave me some money an I had some so when I got ready to go over seas I sent home $60 an I sent home $25 last month an I got paid the first of Jan. So I am going to send home $25 more. Write me when you get time an tell ever body hello. I will be back as soon as we kill the rest of the Jerrys. Lots of Love an Luck
Bud

Jan. 5, 1945
In Germany

Dearest Mama

I wonder what you an all the family are doing today. I am fine an not working very hard. I received 4 letters yesterday. I got 3 from Dot, 1 from Clarise 1 from Bessie 1 from Betty but I didn't hear from you. I hope to hear from you today. Tell them I will answer their letters as soon as I can. Clarise sent me Wills address an I wrote him last night. I hope I hear from him soon. She said in her letter that if I wanted a fruit cake for Christmas to write an let youall know. The letter was mailed the 1 of Nov. An I got it the 4 of Jan. All most two month since it was mailed. Her and Betty and Bessie wrote almost the same thing in there letters. They told me about the wreck at Green Sea.

Sal seems to be dating Bishop right on. She told me about him carrying her to see a high price show. She seemed to enjoy it.

Betty said that . . . .Clark was home again. I guess he is proud to be in the states so he can go home.

Tell Son that I was proud to get his letter an will answer it soon. I can't write anymore now. Will write more pretty soon.
Lots of Love an Luck
Bud
Write the letters air mail so I will get them a lot sooner.

In Germany
Jan. 6, 1945

Dearest Mom

How are you an all the family getting along these winter days. I hope Ralph leg is not any worse that it has been any of the time. I will be glad when I find out how he got it hurt an all about it. Mama I got paid the first of the month and I am going to send it home when I can get a money order. If you ever happen to need it go ahead and use it. But I hope you dont have any bad luck of any kind. I wonder what Ralph doctor will cost. I still havent gotten any more mail. I hoping to get some ever day. Bye an keep sweet.

Lots of Love an Luck
Bud

In Germany
Jan. 6, 1945

Dearest Girls,

How are you all today? I am fine. I received a letter from both of you one day this week and I got 3 from dot that day. I heard from mama an Edna yesterday. One of the letters were written the 20 of Dec an the other was written Christmas. I don't see how I got them so quick. I hope I get my Christmas packages soon. Mama told me in her letter what she got for Dot for a Christmas present. I believe she will like it fine. Edna told me what Hubert gave her for Christmas. I bet Son was proud of the bicycle mama got for him. I hope ralph liked what ever he got for Christmas.

Betty I guess you are enjoying married life fine. I hope you an C. P. gets along as good as me and my last wife did.

Sal I guess you are about to get married. Well I hope you don't get married until I get back to the states. I want to be at your wedding.

Girls I haven't slept with my clothes off but one night since I have been over seas. I don't sleep on sheets since I left . . . . (not legible word).

I would like to write both of you but I don't have time so both of you'll write often an keep sweet.

Lots of Love
BUD

Excuse this German stationary

In Germany

Jan. 7, 1944

Dearest Mama,

How are you an all of the family. I am fine an I hope you all are the same. I have been feeling better the last few days. I have been getting lots of mail. I have gotten 4 letters today an I may get some more tonight. I got 3 from Dot 2 from you 2 from Edna 1 from Betty 1 from Son. Well at last I got the letter that told me how Ralph got his leg hurt. All of the mail that I got today was Nov. mail. You said that you had my pictures back that I had made on furlough. That will be quite a lot of decoration for the house. People will think it is Halloween when they go to our house.

Mama you could never realize how much getting mail can build up my morale. I believe the boys over here would go crazy if they didn't get mail once in a while. Mama I got a letter today an I opened it to read it an it started off (Dearest Darling) an soon as I look at that I decided that it wasn't my mail. But I look on the envelope an it was still mine. I feel big somebody calling me Dearest Darling. Of course it didn't make me mad. Tell all the family that I will write when I get a chance an I hope thats soon. I hope I hear from Vera soon I have written her 3 times since I have been over seas. Tell all of them how glad I was to receive mail from them an for them to keep it up. You asked what kind of weather we were having here. Well we are having lots of snow now but its not to cold. I sure could be lots worse. You said that you didn't guess you could send me a birthday present. Well that's okay. I didn't expect one. You couldn't have sent me one that I could have kept anyway. Mama I don't have anything with me now but a razor an what I have on. I went back last week an took a bath an got clean clothes. I am going to send a money order home as soon as I can get one. An I hope that wont be long. Take care of your self an tell everbody hello. An write soon.

Lots of Luck an Love

BUD

Jan. 9, 1945

Dearest Clarise,

I guess you are surprised to hear from me. I hope you have been getting my mail. I have been writing you all often. I try to write ever chance I get. I don't want you all to think its rough over here for its not. I am getting plenty to eat an have a warm place to sleep. Bye the way I got a shower an some clean clothes last week. I want you to see if you can't stop this war. I believe the germans are about ready to quit fighting anyway. I no we sure are. I am not mad with any body an I don't think its nice to kill. So the sooner this war stops the better it will be for all of us. Some of the boys don't write home often. I guess they have their folks thinking they dont have time that they are fighting to hard. I have just gotten through writing mama, and I sent her a money order for $35.00. I guess I better close and write Dot. I have been getting mail pretty often. I wrote Will one day. I hope I hear from him soon. Excuse this paper. My German stationery is given out.

Lots of Love an Luck

BUD

(The Last Letter)

Jan. 9, 1945
In Germany

Dearest Mama

How are you getting along these cold winter days. I hope you are all fine. I am fine only I have a cold but it isn't very bad. I hope Ralph is getting along fine with his broken leg.

I didn't get any mail today or yesterday but I got enough Sunday to last a few days. I hope you have been getting my mail. I write you ever day. I have been having plenty time lately to write. It has been snowing for the past two days. The snow is about a foot deep now. Mom I am getting along fine. I get plenty to eat and have a warm place to sleep ever night. The time sure pass fast over here. I sure will be glad when the Jerrys surrender. I guess that will be the happiest time of all our life. Son told me in his letter that Roosevelt won the election. I am sending a $35.00 money order home. If you need it use it. I will write again when I can. Write soon and keep sweet and tell ever body hello.

Lots of Love and Luck
BUD

Dont worry about me unless you don't hear from me for about three months for the mail gets captured sometimes.

APPENDIX B

How They Signed the Flag

H. G. Adkins Jr., 14 Barrow St., Rock Hill, S.C.

Pfc Paul S. Allen, Demorest, GA Box 17

Cecil Atkins, Landrum, South Carolina (He did not sign but
   brought the flag home)

Howard R. Bailey 1400 Asheboro ST. Greensboro, N.C.

Jack Belcher, Wellford, S.C.

William M. Bishop Box 94 Taylors, S.C.

Thomas Blackwell Gaffney S.C.

Leo V. Bloom, Baltimore, MD

Sgt. Ray Brown, 625 Indiana Avenue, Hammond, IND

W. Campbell, Evansville, Ind

Bill Carrigan, Taylorville, N.C.

Pfc Roy Clements, Clementsville, Ky

Newton H. Corbitt, Nashville, Tenn

Pfc George R. Decker, Millwood, Ky

Harold G. Ekstrom, Moline, Ill.

Pfc Milton Feldman, 601 West 148th St., New York, N.Y.

Erasmo Garza, 2519 Coleman, Corpus Christi, Texas

Raymond Henke

J.D. Johnson, Spencer, Ind.

Ray Johnson, Poulsbo, WN

S/Sgt. Alfred M. Langberg, 608 Delaware St., Paulsboro, N.J.

Charles Lassiter, High Point, N.C.

William R. Lawless, Piedmont, S.C. R.#1

Bill Leadly, Fort Dodge, Iowa

George Megarry 6319 Parnell, Chicaga ILL

George P. Meadows, 301 Hanover St., Fredericksburg, Va
A.J. Petrella, 723 Michigan, Columbus, Ohio
Paul Shinkevich, 322 E. 10th Str Kewanee, ILL
Maurice Shoemaker Box 39 R1, Lewisburg, Ky
L.F. Simon, Glencoe, MO
Franklin E. Smith, Matlock Route, Shelton, Washington
Pfc Raymond T. Suchomel, 1817 S. 57 Ave Cicero, Illinois
John Thompson, 114 Francis Ave Hartford, Connecticut
Ben F. Travis, Los Angeles, Calif.
James E. Woodhull, Pittsfield, Vermont

NOTES

PROLOGUE

1. A pie safe is a cupboard with doors, usually with pierced tin panels on the front to admit air. The design dates to the eighteenth century and was originally used to store baked items like pies and also perishables such as meat before home refrigeration was available.

2. Those serving with the US government overseas call the newspaper *Stars and Stripes*. The publication has a history dating to the Civil War when Union Troops first printed an edition. The newspaper was revived in World War I for the members of the American Expeditionary Force in Europe in 1918–19. It was revived again in World War II in 1942 and today continues as an independent source of information for American military and government civilians and their families overseas and throughout the United States through the newspaper's online editions. The newspaper is headquartered in Washington, DC, and has editions and staff in Europe and the Pacific. Stripes reporters have covered the US military in all its post–World War II engagements to include, Korea, Vietnam, Bosnia, Africa, the Middle East, and many other locations. The newspaper is a nonappropriated fund organization of the US government with financial support from the Department of Defense. The newspaper has editorial independence as a First Amendment newspaper. I spent most of my twenty-eight-plus years with the European Stars and Stripes as a reporter and eventually chief editor. During that time, I also worked twice as editor of *Pacific Stars and Stripes*. I completed my time at *Stars and Stripes* serving just over a year as worldwide executive editor in Washington, DC.

CHAPTER 1: A SISTER REMEMBERS

1. Betty Blanton Mincey, interview.

2. Horry County school records show Bud Blanton completed the 9th grade in 1940, the year his father died.

3. Mike's Café was a Mullins institution for decades. It was operated by Mike and Anastasia (Stasa) Petros and located on the corner of Main and West Wine Street across from the Mullins Library and a short walk from the Anderson movie theater. Mike was from the island of Rhodes and Anastasia from a Greek village

in Asia Minor. The couple had three daughters: Evelyn Mike, Olga, and Tula. The café was in the east corner of the Old Brick Tobacco Warehouse, which was torn down late in the twentieth century.

CHAPTER 2: FROM THE FARM TO THE FRONT LINE

1. Selective Service was the United States' first peacetime draft law and affected men from the age of 18 to 64. According to Selective Service information, of the 15 million men who served in the US Armed Forces during World War II, approximately 66 percent were drafted.

2. Fletcher Blanton, World War II Draft Cards Young Men, 1940–47. Order number 12174.

3. Betty Blanton Mincey, interview.

4. C. P. Mincey, interview.

5. The 29th landed on Omaha Beach in the first wave on D-Day and suffered heavy casualties. The Big Red One shoulder patch of a red numeral one on an olive drab shield originated in World War I when the division was organized as the First Expeditionary Division. It is also sometimes called the Fighting First or BRO for the Big Red One.

6. Betty Blanton Mincey, interview.

7. Betty Blanton Mincey, interview.

8. The ship's name honored US Marine Corps General John Archer Lejeune, for whom the Marine base, Camp Lejeune at Jacksonville, North Carolina, is named. It was originally commissioned in 1937 as a German passenger ship for the East-Africa Line. It was confiscated by the United States from its interned status in Brazil and moved to Norfolk, Virginia. In 1943, after refitting, it was renamed and began troopship duty in the spring of 1944.

9. Clark, *War Stories of WWII*, 16.

10. Blood, "Christmas Vegetation in Normandy," 24.

11. Nile Robert Blood of West Salem, Illinois, survived the war and completed his degree in civil engineering from the University of Illinois at Urbana. He and his wife Ona Ruth were active for many years in Timberwolf Division reunions. He died in 2002 and his wife in 2013.

12. Marshall, "The Long March," 34.

13. Marshall, "The Long March," 34.

14. Ponzevic, "Into Belgium," 36. Ponzevic, from Chicago, Illinois, died the year the article was published in 2006. He was 82.

15. Vigdor, "Foxhole Manners," 42. Henry Vigdor, from Windsor, Connecticut, went on to earn degrees from New York University and the Hartford Graduate School. According to the *Hartford Courant*, he retired as Assistant Executive Director of Mount Sinai Hospital in Hartford in 1982 and died in 2013 at the age of 88. Brigadier General Bryant E. Moore later commanded the 8th Infantry Division

in Europe. As a major general, he was a corps commander in the Korean Conflict and was killed at the front in Korea after a helicopter crash in February 1951.

CHAPTER 3: THE FIRST YEAR WITHOUT HIM

1. Betty Blanton Mincey, interview.

2. Father Edward Doyle, 1907–97, was a chaplain with the Timberwolf Division in World War II. He later taught at Providence College. He was a member of the Providence College faculty from 1941 to 1954. He served in the division on a leave of absence and was present when Timberwolf soldiers liberated the concentration camp at Nordhausen, Germany. After the war he returned to the teaching faculty. His papers are in an online collection at Father Edward Doyle, O.P. Collection | Providence College Digital Library.

3. I lost contact with Willie Bishop's son Steve who eventually left professional golf to join the staff at the Kennedy Space Center and worked there thirty-six years as a logistics engineer. He died in 2015.

4. The F. W. Woolworth Five-and-Dime was a convenience store prominent in the nineteenth and twentieth centuries with low-cost items. In its day it was similar to modern-day Dollar Stores.

CHAPTER 4: COMING HOME

1. *Florence (SC) Morning News*, Nov. 3, 1948, 5. Reverend Charlie Hill was the Methodist minister in Nichols at the time. After finding the clipping, I learned that Hill was the uncle of longtime Columbia attorney Charles E. Hill, my graduate school roommate at the University of South Carolina. Neither Charles nor I knew of his uncle's connection to my family until I began the research for this book.

2. Nichols Post 82 is the same Legion Post in which C. P. Mincey at 97 was the oldest living member in the summer of 2024.

CHAPTER 5: THOSE HE LEFT BEHIND

1. Williams, "The things we do for LOVE," 36.

2. Wendy Batey, telephone interview.

3. Kimberly Patterson, telephone interview.

CHAPTER 6: BUD BLANTON'S FRIENDS
WHO ALSO NEVER CAME HOME

1. Dud Watts, World War II Draft Cards Young Men, 1940–47. Order number 1102.

2. Private First Class Dud Watts obituary, *Florence (SC) Morning News*, Feb. 8, 1949, 6. The obituary noted that the Reverend Charlie Hill presided at a funeral service at the Watts home and that members of American Legion Post 82 in

Nichols served as pall bearers for the reinterment at Riverside five years after Dud Watts's death in battle.

3. Billy Watts, World War II Draft Cards Young Men, 1940–47. Order number 12250.

4. "Marion County's War Dead at 58," *Florence (SC) Morning News*, July 5, 1946, 3.

5. Henri-Chapelle American Cemetery is two miles northwest of the village of Henri-Chapelle, Belgium, at 159, rue du Mémorial Américain. No record of Billy Watts's reinterment ceremony was available in the *Florence Morning News* or *The State* (Columbia, SC) newspaper, both of which carried the announcement of his death in 1945.

6. Horry County school records show Billy Watts completed the eighth grade in 1942. There is no record of Dud Watts's enrollment at Floyds High School. It is believed he completed Spring Branch Elementary a few miles from the Watts family farm.

7. The Silver Star is the United States military's third highest decoration for valor in combat.

8. US Navy, Cinpac Document 018837.

9. *The State*, Oct. 27, 1944, 4-B.

10. *The News and Courier* (Charleston), Oct. 25, 1948, 2. The article also noted: "Surviving are his parents, Mr. and Mrs. Boyd Ford of Nichols, Route 2; four brothers, Dennie Lancing Ford of the army air corps, Wilton P. Murphy Ford, of Mullins, Corporal Curtis Boyd Ford of Langley field, and Wm. Asburn Ford of Nichols; four sisters Mrs. Quincey Small of Nichols, Miss Ethel Ford of Danville, Va, Miss J.B. Schoolfield of Mount Pleasant, and Mrs. Vaughan McCracken of Columbia."

11. Horry County school records show Forrest Floyd graduated in 1942.

12. *The State* (Columbia, SC), Dec. 17, 1947, 5-A.

13. One of the papers in Forrest's military file shows his unit as Co. D, 87th Infantry Regiment, 10th Mountain Infantry Division. This had to be a mistake. The two divisions had trained together at one point, but the 10th Mountain was fighting in Italy at the time Forrest was killed in Belgium.

14. US Army Personnel file, Forrest Floyd, 19.

15. *Atlanta (GA) Journal-Constitution*, Jan. 16, 1952, 19.

16. US Army Personnel file, Forrest Floyd, 4.

17. Barbara Godfrey Jones obituary, *Myrtle Beach (SC) Sun-News*, Nov. 16, 2013, C-5.

18. Spurgeon Lothair Godfrey, World War II Draft Cards Young Men, 1940–47. Order number 12395A.

19. A paraphrase of the biblical verse in John 15:13.

20. Horry County school records show Leo Huggins completed the 8th grade at Floyds High.

21. Evelyn Huggins Cooke assisted her father Maston in finally getting the records in order listing her mother as deceased. She died in 1999 and is also buried at Riverside Cemetery.

22. Over the course of three decades as a reporter for *Stars and Stripes,* I visited and stayed in the town of Isigny many times while on numerous D-Day commemorative assignments, never knowing until this research that it was close to the place where Leo Huggins fought and died. Isigny today remains a somewhat sleepy village most famous for its naturally salty Normandy butter. In the weeks after D-Day, however, it was a bustling center for US military traffic.

23. La Cambe eventually became a German war cemetery and is distinguished by the black stone crosses that mark the graves of German war dead there. The cemetery is the final resting place for more than 21,000 German service members, and each year remains are found in this battlefield region to add to that total.

24. *The Record* (Columbia), May 22, 1948, 5-B. Sarah Vodie Powell Huggins died May 13, 1944, three weeks before her son Leo's death in combat. Maston Jurd Huggins died in 1952.

25. Betty Floyd Ray, telephone interview.

26. The cemetery was located approximately sixteen miles east of the World War I battle area at St. Mihiel and fifteen miles north of Toul in eastern France. This was about twenty miles northeast of where Hayden's division, the 26th Infantry, had been fighting at the time of his death.

27. US Army Personnel file, Ottis Hayden Floyd, 21.

28. The *News and Courier* (Charleston), Sept. 27, 1948, 2.

29. Ruby Floyd eventually married James Deberry Gibson of Gibson, North Carolina, on Aug. 1, 1948, and they settled first in Clio, South Carolina. She died in 1997 and her husband in 2016.

30. Horry County school records show Hayden Floyd left school in 1941 after completing the eighth grade.

31. Betty Ray finished Floyds High School in 1950, graduated from Winthrop College at Rock Hill, South Carolina, in 1954, and became a teacher. She later earned her masters degree at Appalachian State in counseling and was guidance counselor at Mullins High for nearly three decades. She met lab technician William Ray at Martin's Hospital in Mullins, and they married in 1958. "We were married 46 years . . . before he died," she said. "We have two daughters, Vencie Maxey and Elizabeth Darrel."

32. *The State* (Columbia, SC), May 10, 1945, 6.

33. Frankie Blanton, interview. Frankie Blanton is chief executive officer of Blanton Building Supplies in Horry and Marion counties. He is a former chairman of the Horry County School Board and has been involved in other public service activities throughout his life. His late father James was a South Carolina legislator.

34. Ward and Burns, *The War,* 159.

35. Critics of Clark maintained that he was in a race to take Rome, about thirty miles away, before the D-Day landing a few months later.

36. General Mark Clark later headed the United Nations Command in Korea from 1952 to 1953. He served as president of The Citadel, the South Carolina military college at Charleston, from 1954 to 1965. He died in 1987, the last four-star American officer from World War II.

37. Brittie Blanton Strickland, interview. Horry County school records show Gary Frank Blanton completed the 9th grade in 1940.

38. Mt. Olive is an Horry County crossroads settlement a few miles from Brittie Blanton's family home and three miles from Duford where Floyds High School was originally located. Green Sea Floyds High School was formed as a consolidated school in 1976 and the school compound is about one-half mile from the Mt. Olive crossroad.

39. Brittie Blanton Strickland, interview.

40. "WWII Army Casualties: South Carolina." Fletcher Blanton, Forrest Floyd, Leo Huggins, Billy Watts, and Dud Watts are listed on the casualty list for Marion County. Gary Blanton and Ottis Hayden Floyd are listed on the Horry County casualty register. Lothair Godfrey died after the war ended. Vincent Astor Ford is not listed. He is believed to have had an address outside South Carolina during his long years in military service, and thus would appear on a casualty listing in another state.

CHAPTER 7: PETER BATTY AND THE AMERICAN
MILITARY CEMETERY AT MARGRATEN

1. The second time I was saluted by a border guard was in 1999 at a crossing point between Kosovo and Macedonia during a reporting visit to a conflicted area. There, in the aftermath of NATO's bombing campaign against Serbia, troops of the Kosovo Liberation Army saluted me vigorously after looking at my passport. I had been mistaken for a US diplomatic envoy to the region, William G. Walker. I said nothing as troops waving AK-47s ushered my car ahead of dozens of waiting vehicles and across the border into the relative safety of Macedonia.

CHAPTER 8: FINDING PETER BATTY

1. *The State* (Columbia, SC), Sept. 30, 1973, 2-E.

2. Monika Batty Hörschkes, interview.

3. Evelyn Batty Glasmacher, interview.

4. After Korea, Euel Shelley finished Clemson and had a career as a rural mail carrier in Nichols. He married Mary Ann Townsend of Columbia, and they had three daughters, Beth, Linda, and Charlotte. Euel, 96, and Mary Ann live with daughter Linda at Wagram, North Carolina.

5. Casualty figures show 5,662 Merchant Marine sailors died in World War

II. That total includes 4,780 missing and presumed dead and 845 killed at sea. For additional details, see "Research Starters: US Military by the Number."

6. Cheryl Walker McClellan, email to the author, Feb. 8, 2024.

7. British and American forces carried out the main landing assault on September 9, 1943, near the coastal port of Salerno, which was around and past the Amalfi Coast below the key port city of Naples on the southern coast of Italy. The assault, codenamed Operation Avalanche, ran into unexpected heavy resistance from multiple German divisions defending the coastline. There was a second diversionary landing by British airborne Forces at Taranto, another port 125 miles to the South at the heel of the so-called Italian boot. The Germans put up stiff resistance, and Allied casualties were high at Salerno. The Allies eventually prevailed and took the port of Naples in early October, thus securing the southern part of Italy.

8. Cheryl Walker McClellan, email to the author, Feb. 8, 2024. Sheldon Walker had listed his weight at 160 pounds when he registered for the draft.

9. See Walker, *Rebel Gibraltar,* for a description of the importance of the Confederate fortress at the mouth of the Cape Fear River and its capture by Union troops in the American Civil War.

10. Cheryl Walker McClellan, email to the author, Feb. 10, 2024.

11. Cheryl Walker McClellan, email to the author, Feb. 12, 2024.

12. Cheryl Walker McClellan, email to the author, Feb. 10, 2024.

13. Cheryl Walker McClellan, email to the author, Feb. 12, 2024.

14. James Laurence Walker Jr. email to the author, Aug. 17, 2022, on the occasion of the 51st anniversary of his father's death.

CHAPTER 9: THE TIMBERWOLVES

1. Queck, "The Luck of the Draw," 306. Dallas Reid Queck, originally from Bettendorf, Iowa, survived the war and became an Iowa school teacher and coach in football, boys and girls basketball, track, and baseball. He died in 2014 and is buried at the Sarasota National Cemetery, Sarasota, Florida. He was survived by Rusty Queck, his wife of sixty-six years, and two daughters. Obituary, *Iowa City Press-Citizen*, Oct. 23, 2014, A-4.

2. Ponzevic, "Merry Christmas," 308.

3. See 104th Division Battle Stats.

4. Clark, *War Stories of World War II*, v.

5 104th Infantry Division—Order of Battle of the United States Army—WWII–ETO | US Army Center of Military History Also, Timberwolf Tracks, 380. Army historians record the division as being engaged for 178 days of combat. Hoegh and Doyle in *Timberwolf Tracks* use division statistics which show 195 consecutive days of contact with the enemy before the linkup with the Russians.

6 Infantry Division—National Timberwolf Pups Association.

CHAPTER 10: TWO MEDAL OF HONOR RECIPIENTS, TWO DIFFERENT STORIES

1. "Babette De Fronch Weds Cecil Bolton," *Huntsville (AL) Times,* Dec. 9, 1934, 8.

2. Congressional Medal of Honor Society. President Harry S. Truman presented the Medal of Honor to Bolton on Aug. 23, 1945, at the White House. On that day Truman presented the nation's highest military award to twenty-eight men, including Bolton. All were white. Willie James and six other deserving African American veterans of World War II would have to wait another half century for their moment of national recognition. See Hinnershitz, "Honor Deferred."

3. Vick, "The Story of Cecil H. Bolton." An oak leaf cluster is a ribbon denoting preceding decorations and awards. A bronze cluster represents one additional award (up to four ribbons) and a silver oak leaf cluster is awarded in place of five bronze clusters.

4. Willy F. James Jr., World War II Draft Cards Young Men, 1940–47. Order number S-1904.

5. Guise, "PFC Willy F. James Jr's Medal of Honor," The National WWII Museum, Feb. 28, 2022.

6. Armand J. Serrabella died the following day of his wounds. He was 36. He is buried at the Netherlands American Cemetery in Margraten. Serrabella, from Patchogue, New York, is buried at Plot H Row 9 Grave 12. His decorations included the Silver Star and Purple Heart with Oak Leaf Cluster. Obituary, *Newsday* (Suffolk Edition), May 14, 1945, 3.

7. *Newsday* (Suffolk Edition), May 14, 1945.

8. Willy F. James Jr., Congressional Medal of Honor Society, www.cmohs .org.

9. The commission report was eventually published in book form. See Converse et al., *The Exclusion of Black Soldiers from the Medal of Honor in World War II.* Beyond the systemic failure to recognize the contributions of African American service members in awarding the nation's highest military honor, large groups of Americans failed to recognize, honor, and respect African Americans in uniform. A tragic example of the postwar experience of those soldiers was the case of World War II Black veteran Sergeant Isaac Woodard. In 1946, Woodard, on his way home by Greyhound Bus to Winnsboro, South Carolina, had an argument with the bus driver about his request for the driver to pull over for a bathroom break. Woodard, who was in uniform, was ordered off the bus at the next stop in Batesburg, South Carolina, and taken into custody by town police chief Lynwood Shull. While in custody Woodard was beaten and blinded in a savage attack. Shull was eventually charged with the assault but acquitted by an all-white jury that

deliberated thirty minutes. The Woodard case is detailed in Richard Gergel's 2019 book *Unexampled Courage.*

10. Hinnershitz, "Honor Deferred."

11. "Black WWII Vets Get Medals of Honor," *Omaha World Herald*, Jan. 13, 1997, 1.

12. At Margraten, Lieutenant Colonel Robert Cole is buried at Plot B, Row 15, Grave 27; Private George J. Peters, Plot G, Row 17, Grave 8; Staff Sergeant George Peterson, Plot D, Row 21, Grave 10; Private First Class Walter C. Wetzel, Plot N, Row 18, Grave 10; and First Lieutenant Walter Will, Plot D, Row 3, Grave 32.

13. Retired First Sergeant Robert Gray III, telephone interview.

CHAPTER 11: JAMES GIBSON AND THE HOUSE ON AVERETTE STREET

1. Quang Tri was the northernmost of the South Vietnamese provinces after the 1954 separation of Vietnam into North and South. It was a region of heavy fighting from 1966 onward through the end of 1972. The most notable battle was at Khe Sanh from January to July 1968. At least 274 American servicemen were killed in the half-year battle there and another 2,500 wounded.

2. James's father Noah chose a flat bronze marker from the US Government; it was shipped by the Seaboard Coast Line Railroad to Mullins later in the year and put in place at Riverside Cemetery.

3. Noah Gibson died in 1980. Bertha Beck Gibson died in 1985. Both are buried at Riverside Cemetery near their son James. All but one of the couple's eight daughters survive.

4. National D-Day Memorial at Bedford, Virginia, www.dday.org.

5. Population figures from Virginia Places, www.virginiaplaces.org.

CHAPTER 12: THE NAMES ON A FLAG

1. 1940 Federal Census, Herman Adkins, South Carolina, York County, Rock Hill City, Sheet number 8 A.

2. Herman Guy Adkins Jr., World War II Draft Cards Young Men, 1940–47. Order number 11075.

3. Chicago and North Western Railroad Employment Records, 1035-1970, Herman Guy Adkins Jr. (Rock Hill, South Carolina, birthplace)

4. 1950 Federal Census, Herman G. Adkin Jr., Chicago, Cook County, Sheet number 9. The lack of an s on his surname in the census is presumed to be a writing error by the census taker. He was listed as the head of a single household, with South Carolina as his place of birth.

5. Herman Adkins Jr., obituary, *The Herald* (Rock Hill, SC), Oct. 9, 1972. The newspaper noted: "Surviving are the parents Mr. and Mrs. Herman Adkins Sr. of Rock Hill; two sons, Eddie Adkins of Charlotte, and Donald Adkins of Rock Hill;

a sister, Mrs. A. D. Ford of Knoxville, Tenn.; two brothers, William F. Adkins Sr., and Murray Adkins, both of Rock Hill; eight grandchildren."

6. Hannah Curry Reid obituary, *The Herald* (Rock Hill, SC), May 19, 2010, B-3. Hannah Curry died at age 85. The newspaper noted: "She was married to Herman Guy Adkins, Jr., and Robert A. Reid. Mrs. Reid is survived by sons, Edward R. Adkins Sr. and wife, Sylvia of Monroe, N.C., and Donald R. Adkins of the home; daughters Myra A. Little of Rock Hill, Nancy A. Snead and husband, David, of Clover, SC, and Dianne Thomas and her husband, Michael Parrish, of Catawba, SC; 11 grandchildren, 15 great-grandchildren; and one great-great-grandchild."

7. Herman Adkins obituary, *The State* (Columbia, SC), June 27, 1990, 18.

8. Paul Singleton Allen, World War II Draft Cards, Young Men, 1940–47, Order number 11089.

9. Warren Wayne Allen, telephone interview.

10. Bronze Star Certificate for Private First Class Paul S. Allen in Allen family collection. Also copy of the overall General Orders No. 200-1945 in the Allen collection.

11. Emma Belle Williams Allen obituary service information, *Atlanta (GA) Journal-Constitution*, Feb. 28, 2007, 86. Shawn Allen, Dennis Allen and Wayne Allen were listed as children.

12. An obituary from McGahee-Griffin & Stewart Funeral Home noted: "Paul was a resident of Demorest, Georgia at the time of his passing. He served his country proudly in the United States Army during World War II. He was married to Emma." The obituary added that full military honors would be provided by Grant Reeves VFW Post 7720, Habersham County American Legion Post 84, Rabun County DAV Chapter 95, and the Georgia National Guard. The Allen family received a letter from President Barack Obama honoring his father's service in World War II.

13. Kellie Wallace interview. She explained her relationship to Nora Culbreth Atkins: "she was my great grandmother and she was married to John Henry Atkins Sr. Their sons were William Cecil Atkins and John Henry Atkins Jr. who both were in the war and both returned. William Cecil is my grandfather, my father's (Richard Alvin Atkins Sr.) father. My brother is Richard Alvin Atkins Jr."

14. 1940 Federal Census, William C Atkins, South Carolina, Landrum, Campobello Township, Sheet 15 B.

15. William Cecil Atkins, World War II Draft Cards Young Men, 1940–47. Order number S 1739.

16. Ruth Daniel is listed as the single 19-year-old daughter of rural mail carrier Walter Daniel of Campobello, South Carolina, in the 1940 census for Landrum, Campobello township, sheet 11B.

17. 1950 Federal Census, William C Atkins, Campobello, Spartanburg County, Sheet number 71.

18. William Atkins obituary, *The Greenville News*, Sept. 3, 1976, 14. The newspaper noted that in addition to his wife Ruth, "Surviving also are a son, Richard Atkins of Doraville, Ga.; three sisters, Mrs. Thomas Gosnell of Campobello, Miss Louise Atkins of Landrum and Mrs. D.H. Wright of Spartanburg; a brother, John H. Atkins Jr. of Inman; and two grandchildren."

19. 1930 Federal Census, Howard R. Bailey, North Carolina, Guilford County, Greensboro, Sheet 13B. The census listed two older children, Mimie B. Bailey, 13, and Harry C. Bailey, 18.

20. Howard Ray Bailey, World War II Draft Cards Young Men, 1940–47. Order number S-1573.

21. Jack Belcher, World War II Draft Cards Young Men, 1940–47. Order number S-3299.

22. Jack Belcher obituary, *Greenville (SC) News*, Nov. 19, 1994, 6. His obituary noted: "Surviving are a son, Clifford Belcher of Wellford; a daughter Susan B. Caldwell of State College, Pa.; and two sisters, Mrs. Robert (Jessie) Burdette of Wellford and Louise Willard of Columbia."

23. 1940 Federal Census, William M Bishop, South Carolina, Chick Springs, Greenville County, Taylors, Sheet 2 B.

24. William Manley Bishop, World War II Draft Cards Young Men, 1940–47. Order number S-1136.

25. Thomas Marion Blackwell, World War II Draft Cards Young Men, 1940–47. Order number 2055.

26. 1950 Federal Census, Thomas M Blackwell, South Carolina, Spartanburg County, Sheet 46.

27. Leo Victor Bloom, World War II Draft Cards Young Men, 1940–47. Order number 12,378.

28. Leo V. Bloom, Department of Veterans Affairs BIRLS Death File, 1850–2010.

29. Bloom-Malchowsky wedding, *Baltimore (MD) Sun*, Aug. 26, 1945, 58. The story noted: "Mr. and Mrs. Davis Malchowsky, of Orem avenue, have announced the marriage of their daughter, Miss Annette Machowsky, to Corporal Leo V. Bloom, AUS, son of Mrs. Rose Bloom of Boardman Avenue, and the late Mr. Abraham Bloom. The ceremony was performed July 19 by Rabbi Israel Tabak."

30. Leo V. Bloom obituary, *Evening Sun* (Baltimore, MD), July 30, 1982, 49. The article noted: "The Baltimore native served in the Army during World War II. While in the service he studied engineering at Princeton University . . . He is survived by his wife of 37 years, the former Annette Malchowsky; a daughter, Ava Wyler, of Pikesville, a son Robby Bloom of Pikesville; his brothers Herman Bloom, of Hallandale, Fla., and Morris Bloom, of Surfside, Fla; a sister, Irene Goldstein, of Pikesville and three grandchildren."

31. Annette Bloom Samuels obituary, *Baltimore (MD) Sun*, Feb. 18, 2017, A13. The obituary notes that Annette Bloom Samuels had been married to the late Leo Bloom and Egon Samuels and was the mother of Ava Wyler and Robby Bloom. She was buried at Beth El Memorial Park in Randallstown, MD.

32. Ray John Brown, World War II Draft Cards Young Men, 1940–47. Order number 2249.

33. Ray J Brown, World War II Army Enlistment Records, 1938–46.

34. 1950 Federal Census, Ray J. Brown, Indiana, Lake County, Highland, Sheet number 1.

35. Obituary Ray John Brown, *Vidette-Messenger* of Porter County Indiana, 1972-06-23, 8.

36. Wilfred Howerton Campbell, World War II Draft Cards Young Men, 1940–47. Order number S-2485.

37. Wilfred H. Campbell, Department of Veterans Affairs BIRLS Death File, 1850–2010.

38. Wilfred H. Campbell obituary, *Evansville (IN) Courier & Press*, Sept. 22, 1980, 6. The story noted: "Surviving are his wife, the former Ethel Stevens; sons, Ronald of Texas, and Steve and James, both of Colorado; daughters Mrs. Sandra Leinenbach of Evansville and Mrs. Janet Campbell of Colorado; brothers Herman and Albert Campbell, both of Evansville; sisters Mrs. Ethel Dunn and Mrs. Irma Paul, both of Colorado, and Mrs. Mildred Gibson of Evansville; seven grandchildren and one great-grandchild."

39. Ethel A. Campbell, Find a Grave.

40. Billy Lee Carrigan, World War II Draft Cards Young Men, 1940–47. Order number 10276.

41. Billy Lee Carrigan, North Carolina record of military service card, June 1, 1948.

42. Carrigan, Bill and Lucille Harris, North Carolina, Alexander, US Marriage Records, 1741–2011, 419.

43. Bill Lee Carrigan obituary, *Statesville (NC) Record and Landmark*, Oct. 15, 1974, 6.

44. James Roy Clements, World War II Draft Cards Young Men, 1940–47. Order number 11357.

45. James Roy Clements, Department of Veterans Affairs BIRLS Death File, 1850–2010.

46. 1950 Federal Census, James Roy Clements, Kentucky, Casey County, Sheet number 25.

47. James Roy Clements, Find a Grave, Index, 1600s–present.

48. Mary E. Clements obituary, *The Advocate-Messenger* (Danville, Kentucky), Sept. 4, 1990, 2.

49. Newton Hunter Corbitt obituary, *The Tennessean*, March 30, 1983, 8. The

obituary noted that the honorary pallbearers were the Cutting Room employees at Levi Strauss Manufacturing Company in Centerville, TN.

50. Margaret Catherine Corbitt obituary, *Dickson (TN) Herald*, Oct. 14, 2009, DA4. The obituary noted that she was a retired machine operator at Levi Strauss Manufacturing. The newspaper reported: "her survivors include her sons, Calvin Corbitt and his wife Linda of Hendersonville and Mark Corbitt and his wife, Tammy of Chapmansboro; daughters Janie Chavers of Centerville, Cathey Tidwell of Ashland City and Lori Simpson of Hendersonville. . . ."

51. George Robert Decker, 1950 Federal Census, Grayson, Kentucky, Sheet 15.

52. George Robert Decker obituary, *Courier-Journal* (Louisville, KY), Oct. 13, 1994, 6.

53. Harold Gust Ekstrom, World War II Draft Cards Young Men, 1940-47. Order number 1366. Harold is listed on the Company D, 413th Infantry roster as Harold C. Ekstrom, but this appears to be a typographical error.

54. "Private Harold Ekstrom Marries Miss Jorns At Chicago Church Service," *Rock Island (IL) Argus*, Nov. 30, 1943.

55. Harold Gust Ekstrom, Department of Veterans Affairs BIRLS Death File, 1850–2010.

56. Juanita B. Ekstrom obituary, *Chicago (IL) Tribune*, July 7, 1991, 31.

57. Milton Feldman, World War II Draft Cards Young Men, 1940–47. Order number 3865. As noted, this is a single index card standing alone in the file as image 1167 from the National Archives and Records Administration on the Ancestry.com site. There is a near blank card following as #1168. The date on the card, 10/22/45, is a mystery unless the card was added after the war. The second near blank card has a stamp with Local Board No. 59, 290 Lenox Avenue, New York 27, New York. The Milton Feldman entries for New York City begin with image 1144 and continue to 1204. Each entry usually requires two images.

58. Milton Feldman, World War II Draft Cards Young Men, 1940–47. Order number 1933.

59. Milton Feldman, World War II Draft Cards Young Men, 1940–47. Order number 11373.

60. Milton Maurice Feldman, World War II Draft Cards Young Men, 1940–47. Order number 2307.

61. Milton Feldman, World War II Draft Cards Young Men, 1940–47. Order number 01169

62. Milton Maurice Feldman, World War II Draft Cards Young Men, 1940–47. Order number 12718.

63. Milton Feldman, World War II Draft Cards Young Men, 1940–47. Order number 10171. He listed his father's address as Bklyn, assumed to be Brooklyn.

64. Erasmo Garza, World War II Draft Cards Young Men, 1940–47. Order number 12319.

65. Erasmo Garza, Texas, US Select County Marriage Records, 1837–1965, Nueces County, No. 33487.

66. Erasmo Garza, 1950 Federal Census, Texas, Corpus Christi, Nueces County, Sheet 27.

67. Raymond P. Henke, World War II Draft Cards Young Men, 1940–47. Order number 10142.

68. Henke-Henry wedding, *Buffalo (NY) News*, Jan. 5, 1928, 10.

69. Henke obituary, *Buffalo (NY) News*, April 16, 1956, 8.

70. Doris H. Snyder obituary, *Sun and the Erie County Independent* (Hamburg, NY), Nov. 18, 1999, 6. Her obituary noted that she was survived by her sons, James, Paul, and Ralph and daughters Nancy Bellman and Jeane D. Hawthorne plus eighteen grandchildren and many great-grandchildren.

71. Joy D. Johnson and Olive Ann Arthur wedding announcement, *Indianapolis Star*, Aug. 5, 1945, 46 and Find A Grave, Joy D. Johnson.

72. Joy D. Johnson obituary, *Reporter-Times* (Martinsville, IN), June 23, 1980, 3.

73. Ray Johnson obituary, *Kitsap Sun* (Bremerton, WA), April 13, 2010, 5.

74. Raymond S. Johnson, World War II Draft Cards Young Men, 1940–1947. Order number 84.

75. Ray S. Johnson, World War II Army Enlistment Records, 1938–46.

76. Alfred Merrill Langberg, World War II Draft Cards Young Men, 1940 1947. Order number 11790.

77. Index of Marriages in New Jersey 1945, Miller.

78. "Miss Hilda Miller Becomes Bride of Alfred Langberg," *Courier-Post* (Camden, NJ), July 12, 1945, 18.

79. Find a Grave provides the following information about Alfred Langberg: "Under the ROTC program, he graduated from Drexel University with a degree in Mechanical Engineering and served in the US Army during World War II in Europe as a Staff Sergeant."

80. Charles Herman Lassiter, World War II Draft Cards Young Men, 1940–47. Order number 3473.

81. Charles H. Lassiter, Army serial number 34439225. His enlisted status like all others was "for the duration of the War or other emergency, plus six months, subject to the discretion of the President or otherwise according to law."

82. 1950 Federal Census, Charles H. Lassiter, North Carolina, High Point, North Carolina, Sheet 15.

83. Charles H. Lassiter, North Carolina, US, Death Indexes, 1908–2004. According to the report he died at the Veterans Hospital in Salisbury, North Carolina.

84. 1940 Federal Census, Ralph Lawless, Anderson County, Williamston Township, Sheet 2A.

85. William Ralph Lawless, World War II Draft Cards Young Men, 1940–47. Order number 11656.

86. Ralph Lawless Sr. obituary, *Greenville (SC) News*, April 15, 1999, 20. His military personnel file (Army Serial Number 3466492654) lists his enlistment date as October 1945 in San Luis Obispo, California, but the date was probably incorrectly entered since the signers are thought to have put their names on the flag sometime in mid-1945. He is also listed on the 413th Regiment Company D World War II roster on which nearly all the other signers appear.

87. Sgt. William R. Lawless Jr. obituary, *Greenville (SC) News*, Jan. 15, 1967, 40. Binh Duong province is in the southeast part of Vietnam. It is about twelve miles north of Ho Chi Minh City, formerly Saigon.

88. Doris Lawless obituary, *Anderson (SC) Independent-Mail*, Sept. 16, 2015, 8. The obituary noted that Doris Lawless was survived "by son, Ronnie Lawless (Lynn) of Williamston; daughter Deborah Simmons (Virgil) of Pelzer; sisters Pearl Schilling of Columbia and Bobbie Sue Faulkner of Charleston; eight grandchildren; fourteen great-grandchildren; Robin Hendricks and Juanita Cape, both raised in the home."

89. His Iowa birth certificate (74-460) lists his birthplace as the township of Ellington in Palo Alto County.

90. School Yearbooks, Ft. Dodge High School 1942. The yearbook indicates he took courses in English, Industrial Arts, Social Science, and Physical Education.

91. Bill Dean Leadley, World War II Draft Cards Young Men, 1940–47. Order number 11491.

92. Marriage listing, *Des Moines Tribune*, Feb. 3, 1948, 14.

93. William D Leadley, 1950 Federal Census, Iowa, Fort Dodge, Iowa 94-41.

94. Billy Dean Leadley, Find a Grave. Birth July 1, 1922, death April 6, 2010. The gravestone which Leadley shares with his wife Shirley spells his name as Billie D. Leadley.

95. George E. Megarry, World War II Draft Cards Young Men, 1940–47. Order number 10896.

96. June Alma Mathews and George E. Megarry, Cook County, Illinois Marriage Index, 1930–60, File number 2067536.

97. 1950 Federal Census, George F. Megarry, Illinois, Cook County, Chicago, Sheet number 14. Even though the record shows George F. MeGarry, this almost certainly is George E. Megarry; his wife is listed as June Alma Megarry.

98. George Parker Meadows, World War II Draft Cards Young Men, 1940–47. Order number 10,968.

99. George P. Meadows and Edna M. Heenan, Certificate of Marriage, Commonwealth of Virginia, Dec. 23, 1948, number 35038.

100. Edna Heenan and George P. Meadows wedding, *Richmond (VA) News Leader*, Jan. 5, 1949, 16.

101. George P. Meadows obituary, *Richmond (VA) Times-Dispatch*, April 14, 1995, 20.

102. Edna Meadows obituary, *Richmond (VA) Times-Dispatch*, Jan. 8, 2014, B6. The obituary noted that she was survived by her son, George Parker Meadows Jr., daughter Shirley Trible, and six grandchildren.

103. Adam John Petrella, World War II Draft Cards Young Men, 1940–47. Order number 771.

104. Adam J. Petrella, Headstone Applications for Military Veterans, 1969.

105. Paul Shinkevich, World War II Draft Cards Young Men, 1940–47. Order number 1598.

106. 1950 Federal Census, Paul Shinkevich. Illinois, Kewanee, Henry County, Sheet number 5.

107. Paul Shinkevich obituary, *The Dispatch* (Moline, IL), Aug. 21, 1989, 8. The obituary added: "Survivors include sisters Stephanie Shurnis, Kewanee, Mary Creasey, Toulon, and Alice Stontz, Moline; brothers, Nicholas and his twin, Peter, both of Kewanee, and Stephen, San Jose, Calif."

108. Paul Shinkevich obituary, Find A Grave.

109. Maurice R. Shoemaker, World War II Draft Cards Young Men, 1940–47. Order number 1598.

110. Maurice R. Shoemaker, Kentucky, Department of Veterans Affairs BIRLS Death File, 1850–2010.

111. Stuart-Shoemaker wedding announcement, *News-Democrat and Leader* (Russellville, KY), January 10, 1946, 4.

112. 1950 Federal Census, Maurice Ryan Shoemaker, Kentucky, Logan, Gordonsville, Sheet 4. The census taker lists him as Morris R. Shoemaker, but all the information about him matches the information for Maurice Ryan Shoemaker, including his wife Elizabeth and son Jerry, both of whom are listed in his obituary.

113. Maurice Ryan Shoemaker, 75, obituary, *News-Democrat and Leader* (Russellville, KY), Sept. 5, 1997, 8. His obituary noted: "He is survived by his wife Elizabeth Shoemaker of Jeffersonville, Ind.; three sons, Jerry Shoemaker of Bowling Green, Ronald Shoemaker of Clarksville, Ind., Keith Shoemaker of Jeffersonville, Ind.; one daughter Pam Shoemaker Abell of New Albany, Ind.; one brother, Tommy Shoemaker of Russellville; four sisters, Mona Williams and Jamie Cauley, both of Lewisburg, Marian Lehman of Pontiac, Mich., and Laura Nell Jessup of Centreville, Ohio; and six grandchildren."

114. Lester Fred Simon, World War II Draft Cards Young Men, 1940–47. Order number S-2126.

115. Lester Fred Simon and Ruby Broemmelsick, Marriage application 1131, St. Louis, 1942.

116. Simon-Broemmelsick marriage notice, *St. Louis (MO) Post-Dispatch*, June 14, 1942, 24.

117. Lester F. Simon, World War II Hospital Admission Card Files, 1942–54.

118. 1950 Federal Census, Lester F. Simon, Missouri, St. Louis (Meramec) 95-369, Sheet 7.

119. Section 1n Site 1461 in the cemetery.

120. Funeral Notices, *St. Louis (MO) Post-Dispatch*, July 7, 2000, B5. The newspaper obituary staff explained that the US flag was included with the death information on all veterans.

121. Ruby Broemmelsick Simon obituary, *St. Louis (MO) Post-Dispatch*, Sept. 19, 2015, A013. She died on Sept. 16, 2015, at the age of 92. Her obituary noted: "Loving wife of the late Lester F. Simon; mother of Linda Sherron and Donald (Lois) Simon; grandmother of Eric Sherron, Beth (Ryan) Humbarger, Kelly (Tim) Schoenmehl and Patrick Simon; great grandmother of Alexandra, Evelyn Brody and Beckett; sister of Ruth Kiefer; aunt, great aunt and friend to many."

122. 1930 Federal Census, Franklin Smith, Washington, Shelton, Sheet 3B.

123. 1940 Federal Census, Franklin E. Smith, Washington, Shelton, Sheet 5A.

124. Franklin Ernest Smith, World War II Draft Cards Young Men, 1940–47. Order number 10910.

125. Frank E. Smith and Louise D. Fish, Washington, US Marriage Records, 1854–2013, 450, Marriage Affidavit Record N. 10.

126. Franklin Smith (born July 2, 1922), US Public Records Index, 1950–93, Vol. 2.

127. 1950 Federal Census, Franklin E. Smith, Washington, Mason County, Sheet 24.

128. Sandra Marie (Smith) Young Eberle obituary, *The Olympian* (Olympia, WA), Nov. 17, 2015, A10.

129. Raymond T. Suchomel, World War II Draft Cards Young Men, 1940–47. Order number 11876.

130. Raymond T. Suchomel, Department of Veterans Affairs BIRLS Death File, 1850–2010.

131. *Chicago Tribune* online, July 4, 2004, and Hitzeman Funeral Home & Cremation Services, Brookfield, Illinois. The Hitzeman obituary noted that he was the father of Pamela R. Dwyer and Jeffrey R. Suchomel. The obituary noted that the Suchomels left behind seven grandchildren and one great grandchild. See also *Chicago (IL) Tribune*, July 4, 2004, 4–9.

132. *Chicago (IL) Tribune*, May 5, 2013, 1–32.

133. John S. Thompson, World War II Draft Cards Young Men, 1940–47. Order number 11960.

134. John S. Thomson, Department of Veterans Affairs BIRLS Death File, 1850–2010.

135. 1950 Federal Census, John S. Thomson, Connecticut, Newington, Hartford, Sheet 21.

136. John S. Thomson obituary, *Hartford (CT) Courant*, Sept. 14, 1989, 275.

137. Benjamin Franklin Travis, World War II Draft Cards Young Men, 1940–47, Order number 11,067. He was born Dec. 7, 1923, in Delaware, Oklahoma.

138. California, US Death Index, 1940–97, Frank Benjamin Travis. Although the first and last names are transposed, the death date of Dec. 7, 1923, and Oklahoma for his birthplace match.

139. Benjamn Franklin Travis, World War II Draft Cards Young Men, 1940–47, Order number S-3932.

140. Bennington, VT, Birth Certificate, Woodhull, James Edward. His father's occupation was listed as physician.

141. James Edward Woodhull and Norma Falby, Marriage License, June 23, 1940, Pittsfield, Vermont.

142. James Edward Woodhull, World War II Draft Cards Young Men, 1940–47. Order number 298.

143. General Orders 26 October 1945, Headquarters 104th Infantry Division, Camp Luis Obispo, California, Number 200. A copy of the document was obtained from the family of Paul Allen, another signer of the captured flag. Both Woodhull and Allen were announced as Bronze Star recipients on the division order.

144. Florida, US Divorce Index, 1927–2001, James Edward Woodhull and Norma F. Woodhull, Dade, Florida, certificate number 193.

145. James Woodhull obituary, *Washington Post*, April 11, 1996. Courtesy Woodhull Genealogy obituaries.

EPILOGUE: REST EASY, MEN

1. After World War II, the western half of Germany was split into British, French, and American Zones of Occupation. The Eastern half was occupied by the Soviet Army. Berlin, which lay inside the boundary of the new communist East Germany, was divided into the French, British, and American Zones in West Berlin, and the Soviet Zone which was essentially the Eastern half of the former German capital. At the Potsdam Conference in July 1945, the Allies agreed to a program for demilitarization, democratization, and denazification of Germany. The Americans, British, and French worked together in carrying out that program in what became West Germany or the Bundesrepublik Deutschland. In the East the Soviets enforced strict communist rule and founded East Germany, the Deutsche Demokratishe Republik.

2. From the square you could see the nearby TV tower that had become famous, because on clear days the reflection of the sun on the side of the bulbous sphere (below the antenna spire) created a shiny cross. This was a public embarrassment for the East German government, which was officially atheist.

3. "Berlin '89, Hammers of Freedom, Smiles of Hope," *European Stars and Stripes*, Nov. 29, 1989, 14–15. I began the article with this sentence: "The sound of freedom is the ring of a thousand hammers pounding the Berlin Wall."

4. Brian S. Brooks, email to the author, Feb. 17, 2024. Brooks is the author of *Sergeant Shedd.*

5. Meals Ready To Eat (MREs) are the military packets providing a full meal to soldiers in the field. A SOPAKCO plant in Mullins, South Carolina, prepares MREs for distribution all around the world. The hillside on which the soldier and I sat became part of the NATO military base named Camp Bondsteel. The thousand-acre site was named for US Army Staff Sergeant James M. Bondsteel, a Medal of Honor recipient from the Vietnam War. Today it is home to the Kosovo Force tasked with keeping peace in Kosovo.

BIBLIOGRAPHY

NEWSPAPERS

Advocate-Messenger (Danville, KY)
Anderson (SC) Independent-Mail
Atlanta (GA) Journal-Constitution
Bakersfield (CA) Californian
Baltimore (MD) Sun
Buffalo (NY) News
Burlington (Vermont) Free Press
Chicago (IL) Tribune
Columbia (SC) Record
Courier-Journal (Louisville, KY)
Courier-Post (Camden, NJ)
Des Moines (IA) Tribune
Dickson (TN) Herald
European Stars and Stripes (Darmstadt, Germany*)*
The Dispatch (Moline, IL)
Evansville (IN) Courier and Press
Evening Sun (Baltimore, MD)
Florence (SC) Morning News
Greenville (SC) News
Hartford (CT) Courant
Herald (Rock Hill, SC)
Huntsville (AL) Times
Indianapolis (IN) Star
Iowa City (IA) Press-Citizen
Kitsap Sun (Bremerton, WA)
Messenger-Inquirer (Owensboro, KY)
Myrtle Beach (SC) Sun-News
Newsday (Melville, NY)
News and Courier (Charleston, SC)
News-Democrat and Leader (Russellville, KY)

Olympian (Olympia, WA)
Omaha (NE) World Herald
Reno (NV) Gazette-Journal
Reporter Times (Martinsville, IN)
Richmond (VA) News Leader
Richmond (VA) Times-Dispatch
Rock Island (IL) Argus
The State (Columbia, SC)
Statesville Record and Landmark (Statesville, NC)
St. Louis (MO) Post-Dispatch
Sun and the Erie County Independent (Hamburg, NY)
Tennessean (Nashville, TN)
Vidette-Messenger of Porter County (Indiana)
Washington (DC) Post
Wichita (KS) Eagle

DATABASES AND WEBSITES

104th Division Battle Stats, https://history.army.mil/documents/eto-ob/104id-eto
.htm
104th Infantry Division—National Timberwolf Pups Association, www.timber
wolf104inf.org/index.html
1930 Federal Census
1940 Federal Census
1950 Federal Census
Ancestry.com
"The Bedford Boys," National D-Day Memorial, https://www.dday.org/learn
/about-the-memorial-and-bedford/
Chicago and North Western Railroad Employment Records
Congressional Medal of Honor Society, www.cmohs.org
Cook County, Illinois Marriage Index, 1930–60, https://www.ancestry.com/search
/collections/1500/
Department of Veterans Affairs BIRLS Death File, 1850–2010, https://www.fold3
.com/publication/848/us-veterans-affairs-birls-death-file-1850–2010
Find a Grave, findagrave.com
Florida, US Divorce Index, 1927–2001, https://www.ancestry.com/search/collec
tions/8837/
Horry County School Records
The National WWII Museum https://www.nationalww2museum.org/
Newspapers.com
"Research Starters: US Military by the Number, National World War II Museum,"
www.nationalww2museum.org

US Army Personnel Files

US Marriage Records, 1854–2013, https://www.ancestry.com/search/collections/2378/

US Public Records Index, 1950–93

Virginia Places, www.virginiaplaces.org

World War II Draft Cards Young Men, 1940–47

"WWII Army Casualties: South Carolina," National Archives, Military Records, www.archives.gov/research/military/ww2/

INTERVIEWS

Betty Blanton Mincey, interview by the author, November 10, 2022.

Betty Floyd Ray, interview by the author, December 28, 2022.

Brittie Blanton Strickland, interview by the author, January 18, 2023.

C. P. Mincey, interview by the author, November 10, 2022.

Frankie Blanton, interview by the author, December 12, 2022.

Kimberly Patterson, interview by the author, January 12, 2022.

Robert Gray III, First Sergeant (Ret.), interview by the author, February 17, 2024.

Warren Wayne Allen, interview by the author, March 16, 2023.

Kellie Wallace, interview by the author, Jan. 15, 2024.

Wendy Batey, interview by the author, January 22, 2023.

Monika Batty Hörschkes, interview by the author, Feb. 23, 2024.

Evelyn Batty Glasmacher, interview by the author, March 9, 2024.

SECONDARY SOURCES

Blood, Nile R. "Christmas Vegetation in Normandy." In *War Stories of WWII*, edited by Katherine P. Clark, 24. Self-published, 2011.

Brooks, Brian S. *Sergeant Shedd: His Adventures in The Great War*. Columbia, MO: Author, 2017.

Chronister, Paul. "The Egg & I." In *War Stories of WWII*, edited by Katherine P. Clark, 457. Self-published, 2011.

Clark, Katherine P., ed. *War Stories of WWII*. Self-published, 2011.

Converse III, Elliott V., Daniel K. Gibran, John A. Cash, Robert K. Griffith, Jr., Richard H. Kohn. *The Exclusion of Black Soldiers from the Medal of Honor in World War II*. Jefferson, NC: McFarland & Co., 1997.

Gergel, Richard. *Unexampled Courage: The Blinding of SGT. Isaac Woodard and the Awakening of President Harry S. Truman and Judge J. Waties Waring*. New York: Sarah Crichton Books, 2019.

Graff, Richard S. "Refugees and POWs." In *War Stories of WWII*, edited by Katherine P. Clark, 473–474. Self-published, 2011.

Guise, Kim. "PFC Willy F. James Jr.'s Medal of Honor." National WWII Museum. https://www.nationalww2museum.org.

Hinnershitz, Stephanie. "Honor Deferred: Black Veterans and the Medal of Honor." National WWII Museum. https://www.nationalww2museum.org.

Kershaw, Alex. *The Bedford Boys*. Cambridge: Da Capo Press, 2004.

Livingston, Carl, Jr. "A Few Words about Memories." In *War Stories of WWII*, edited by Katherine P. Clark, 413, self-published.

Marshall, Paul. "The Long March." In *War Stories of WWII*, edited by Katherine P. Clark, 34, Self-published, 2011.

Miller, Frank L. "Medic in Battle—Soldier of Mercy." In *War Stories of WWII*, edited by Katherine P. Clark, 495, Self-published, 2011.

Miller, John. "Personal Memories." In *War Stories of WWII*, edited by Katherine P. Clark, 519-520, Self-published, 2011.

Perozzi, Frank J. "Notes and Remembrances." In *War Stories of WWII*, 59, edited by Katherine P. Clark, Self-published, 2011.

Ponzevic, Daniel E. "Into Belgium." In *War Stories of WWII*, 36, edited by Katherine P. Clark, Self-published, 2011.

Ponzevic, Daniel. "Merry Christmas." In *War Stories of WWII*, edited by Katherine P. Clark, 308. Self-published, 2011.

Queck, Dallas R. "The Luck of the Draw." In *War Stories of WWII*, edited by Katherine P. Clark, 306. Self-published, 2011.

Ravnholt, Eiler. "Easter Sunday Memories." In *War Stories of WWII*, edited by Katherine P. Clark, 438-39. Self-published, 2011.

Ritzer, Edward L. "Recollections While In The Service." *War Stories of WWII*, edited by Katherine P. Clark, 45. Self-published, 2011.

Robinson, Forrest J. "Unusual Experience." In *War Stories of WWII*, edited by Katherine P. Clark, 436. Self-published, 2011.

Robinson, Forrest J. "VE Day in Delitzsch." In *War Stories of WWII*, edited by Katherine P. Clark, 480. Self-published, 2011.

Spencer, O.B. "A Bit Too Fast." In *War Stories of WWII*, edited by Katherine P. Clark, 464. Self-published, 2011.

Vick, John. "The Story of Cecil H. Bolton, 1st Lieutenant, US Army WWII, Medal of Honor." *The Andalusia Star News*, January 1, 2021.

Vigdor, Henry. "Foxhole Manners." In *War Stories of WWII*, edited by Katherine P. Clark, 42. Self-published, 2011.

Walker, James Laurence, Jr. *Rebel Gibraltar: Fort Fisher and Wilmington, CSA*. Wilmington, NC: DramTree Books, 2005.

Walker, William S. "Berlin '89, Hammers of Freedom, Smiles of Hope." *European Stars and Stripes*. November 29, 14-15.

Ward, Geoffery C., and Ken Burns. *The War*. New York: Alfred A. Knopf, 2007.

Waterman, Gerald, "A War Story." In *War Stories of WWII*, edited by Katherine P. Clark, 380-81, self-published, 2011.

Williams, Beth. "The Things We Do For LOVE." *South Carolina Magazine*, January 2007, 36.

Wood, Robert E. "The First Day In Combat." (part 2) In *War Stories of WWII*, edited by Katherine P. Clark, 56. Self-published, 2011.

Zipper, Seymour. "Story of a Holocaust Liberator." In *War Stories of WWII*, edited by Katherine P. Clark, 446–47. Self-published, 2011.

INDEX

Page numbers in *italics* indicate illustrative material.